陕西社科丛书

两汉三国历史文化典故悦读

WHISPERS OF ANCIENT DYNASTIES: ENCHANTED TALES OF THE HAN AND THREE KINGDOMS

英汉对照

李俊丽／著

陕西新华出版

陕西人民教育出版社

·西安·

图书在版编目（CIP）数据

两汉三国历史文化典故悦读 / 李俊丽著. —— 西安：
陕西人民教育出版社，2024.8
ISBN 978-7-5450-9516-6

Ⅰ.①两… Ⅱ.①李… Ⅲ.①中国历史—汉代—三国
时代—通俗读物 Ⅳ.①K234.09 ②K236.09

中国国家版本馆 CIP 数据核字(2023)第 182572 号

两 汉 三 国 历 史 文 化 典 故 悦 读

LIANG-HAN SAN-GUO LISHI WENHUA DIANGU YUEDU

李俊丽　著

出版发行		陕西人民教育出版社
地　　址		西安市丈八五路 58 号
邮　　编		710077
经　　销		各地新华书店
印　　刷		陕西金和印务有限公司
开　　本		787 毫米 × 1092 毫米　1/16
印　　张		15
字　　数		202 千字
版　　次		2024 年 8 月第 1 版
印　　次		2024 年 8 月第 1 次印刷
书　　号		ISBN 978-7-5450-9516-6
定　　价		48.00 元

前　言 / Foreword

汉中，位于陕西省西南部，北依秦岭，南屏巴山，因汉水而得名。汉水，又名汉江，古称沔水，发源于汉中境内的宁强县。滔滔不绝的汉江流经汉中盆地，向东奔向长江。汉中因汉江成为南水北调中线工程的重要水源涵养地。汉中，是关中地区与西南地区的重要枢纽，因处于特殊的地理位置，历来是兵家必争之地。尤其是在两汉三国时期，连年征战在这里留下了众多的历史遗迹和人文典故，其中的成语典故更是不胜枚举。硝烟散去，留下来的历史故事、成语典故等成为宝贵的财富。两汉三国的历史也成就了最美汉中。现在的汉中，物产丰富，生态优良，为朱鹮、羚牛、大熊猫、金丝猴等秦岭四宝提供了良好的栖息环境，是国家历史文化名城和中国优秀旅游城市。

Hanzhong, located in the southwest of Shaanxi Province, is surrounded by the Qinling Mountains to the north and the Ba Mountains to the south. It is named after the Han River, which was also known as the Hanjiang or Mianshui in ancient times. The source of the Han River is in Hanzhong's Ningqiang County. It flows through the Hanzhong Basin, and heads eastward towards the Changjiang River. Hanzhong is an important water source for the "South-to-North Water Diversion Project". Hanzhong has played a vital role throughout history as a link between the Guanzhong region and the southwest region. Its strategic location has made it a highly coveted battleground; this was particularly the case during the Western Han, Eastern Han, and Three Kingdoms Periods. The conflicts during those eras left in their wake a wealth of historical stories, cultural allusions,idiomatic expressions,etc.Its rich history, particularly during the Western Han, Eastern Han, and Three Kingdoms Periods, has bestowed upon Hanzhong the captivating allure. Today, Hanzhong boasts abundant natural resources and the pristine ecological environment. It is home to the four treasures of the Qinling Mountains: the crested ibis, the antelope, the giant panda, and the golden monkey. Hanzhong has earned nationwide acclaim as a city of historical and cultural significance, and has become a top tourist destination in China.

　　两汉三国时期是我国重要的历史时期,汉中在当时有着举足轻重的地位。汉高祖刘邦屯兵汉中,"明修栈道,暗度陈仓",取三秦而定天下。三国时期,这块"栈阁北来连陇蜀,汉川东去控荆吴"的战略要地上,曾演绎了多少惊天动地的英雄故事。魏蜀吴相争之时,汉中成为刘备北伐曹魏的军事基地,又是魏灭蜀并吴的军事要地。同时,张鲁也在汉中称过王,创建了五斗米教,建立了我国历史上最早的政教合一政权。魏蜀两大政治势力在这里激烈碰撞,于是就有了老将黄忠定军山下刀劈夏侯渊、一身是胆赵云汉水之滨大败曹军的激烈场面,也留下了曹操褒谷口杀杨修、马岱虎头桥斩魏延的历史悲剧。还有中华民族智慧的化身、一代名相诸葛亮在汉中度过了他一生最为呕心沥血的岁月。为辅佐刘备灭曹复汉,他在汉中屯兵八年,六出祁山,北伐曹魏,鞠躬尽瘁,最终葬于汉中勉县定军山下。其安息地武侯墓的汉柏、汉桂相映成趣。后由刘禅下诏修建的武侯祠被称为"天下第一武侯祠"。品三国必游汉中,在汉中你可以游览古汉台、拜将坛、古虎头桥、石门水库、褒斜栈道、武侯墓、武侯祠、定军山古战场、天荡山古战场、张良庙、马超墓、刘备称汉中王设坛处、诸葛亮读书台、诸葛亮制木牛流马处等久负盛名的景点,尽情领略三国文化的魅力。

The historical significance of Hanzhong during the Eastern Han, Western Han, and Three Kingdoms Periods cannot be overstated. It was here that Liu Bang—Emperor Gaozu during the Han Dynasty—established his empire. He stationed his troops in this region and employed strategies to secure victory over the three Qin generals. One of those strategies was "mending the plank roads while secretly crossing the Chencang". During the Three Kingdoms Periods, Hanzhong played a pivotal role as a strategic location for military campaigns. It became a primary base for Liu Bei's northern campaigns and subsequently served as the base for the Wei Kingdom to conquer Shu Kingdom and Wu Kingdom. Zhang Lu declared himself King Hanzhong in this region and founded the earliest theocratic regime in Chinese history: the Wudoumi Daoist movement (The Way of the Five Pecks of Rice). Legendary events were witnessed during the clashes between the Wei and Shu political forces in Hanzhong. Huang Zhong saw a momentous victory over Xiahou Yuan in the Dingjun Mountain; Zhao Yun gave valiant resistance against Cao Cao's forces along the Han River; and there staged two major tragic episodes: Cao Cao killed Yang Xiu in the Bao Valley, and Ma Dai slayed Wei Yan on the Hutou Bridge. Zhuge Liang, the embodiment of Chinese wisdom, also spent his most arduous years in Hanzhong. He stationed his troops in Hanzhong for eight years and assisted Liu Bei in his mission to overthrow Cao Cao and restore the Han Dynasty. Zhuge Liang launched several expeditions to Mount Qi and led several northern campaigns against Cao Wei. His final resting place, the Martial Marquis Tomb in Mianxian County in Hanzhong, is surrounded by majestic cypress and osmanthus trees. The Martial Marquis Memorial Temple was constructed at the order of Liu Shan, and hailed the "World's Most Prominent Martial Marquis Temple". For those interested in exploring the historical and cultural heritage of the Three Kingdoms, Hanzhong offers many tourist attractions. Visitors can see the ancient Hantai, Baijiang Alter, Hutou Bridge, Stone Gate Reservoir, Bao-Xie Plank Road, Martial Marquis Tomb, Martial Marquis Memorial Temple, the ancient battlefields of the Dingjun and Tiandang Mountains, Zhang Liang's Temple, Ma Chao's Tomb, the altar where Liu Bei was proclaimed King of Hanzhong, Zhuge Liang's Reading Platform, and the site where Zhuge Liang invented the ingenious transport machine "wooden oxen and running horses".

激荡的历史给汉中留下了许多脍炙人口的故事、传说,还有耳熟能详的成语典故。这些故事、传说和成语典故或者是发生在这里,或者是与这里的历史人物有关,比如"明修栈道,暗度陈仓"、萧规曹随、"一人得道,鸡犬升天"、乐不思蜀、廉泉让水,等等。它们的故事性很强,同时简洁明了,也富有哲思,成为中华传统文化的重要符号。文化需要传承,也需要交流。本书以两汉三国时期作为时间维度,以汉中作为地域维度,讲述发生在其间的历史故事、成语典故,在释义的基础上对故事的背景、演进、启示等进行了阐释;同时,将历史故事和成语典故进行戏剧改编,为它们注入新的元素,以消除时间跨度带给人们的疏离感,使之更加贴近生活,更好地传承中华优秀传统文化。在极速发展的新媒体时代,通过戏剧改编的方式宣传推广地方文化和中华优秀传统文化,是一种有益的尝试和探索,为讲好中国故事开辟了一条新的路径,为普及中华优秀传统文化开创了全新的实践教育模式。

The rich history of Hanzhong has given rise to many fascinating stories, legends, and idiomatic expressions. They are closely intertwined with the historical figures and events of Hanzhong. Well-known expressions include "mending the plank roads while secretly crossing the Chencang", "following established rules", "when a man succeeds, all his friends and relatives get favor", "indulge in pleasures and forget home", and "the Lianquan River and Rang River". They offer concise yet profound philosophical insights and serve as important symbols of Chinese traditional culture. It is necessary to preserve and exchange culture. This book delves into the historical stories and idiomatic expressions that came about during the Eastern and Western Han Dynasties and the Three Kingdoms Periods. Hanzhong, renowned for its scenic beauty, is taken as its backdrop. The book provides interpretations of stories and idioms, sheds light on their background, evolution, and inspiration. It also provides examples of dramatic adaptations of these historical stories and idiomatic expressions. By injecting new elements into these narratives, the book bridges the gap between the past and present, and makes historical stories and idiomatic expressions more accessible to readers today. This approach aims to help readers better inherit and promote fine traditional Chinese culture. In an era of fast-growing new media, it is a valuable way of promoting local culture and fine traditional Chinese culture with dramatic adaptations, and it is worth exploring. It opens up a new way of telling Chinese narratives and is a practical way of popularizing fine traditional Chinese culture.

目 录 / Contents

Chapter Five

Theatrical Delights: Idioms from the Western Han, Eastern Han, and Three Kingdoms

第一章
Chapter One

两汉成语典故悦读

Enchanting Tales of Idioms from the Eastern and Western Han Dynasties

筑坛拜将

The Baijiang Alter —The Ritual for Appointing a Commander-in-Chief

1.成语故事 The Story of the Idiom

楚汉相争之时,韩信离开项羽投奔刘邦,希望能够得到刘邦的重用,然而事与愿违。韩信非常失望,就从南郑(今汉中市)离开汉营。萧何素闻韩信大名,认为他是"国士无双"。听到韩信出走的消息后,萧何深恐失去人才,来不及禀报刘邦就急忙连夜去追,最终在凤凰山(今汉中市留坝县马道镇北侧)下追上并成功劝回韩信。这也就是"萧何月下追韩信"的故事。萧何追回韩信后就把他郑重推荐给刘邦,并告诉刘邦:如果您只是打算长期在汉中称王的话,可以不用韩信;但如果您想与项羽争夺天下的话,再也没有比韩信更合适的帮手了。刘邦说看在萧何的面子上就让韩信做个将军,然而萧何建议封韩信为大将军,并且还必须要举行隆重的仪式。刘邦最后听取了萧何的建议,选择良辰吉日,设立高坛,举行了隆重的仪式,任命韩信为大将军统帅兵马。承命之后,韩信率兵四处征伐,为汉王朝的建立立下了汗马功劳。汉中市内的拜将台就是筑坛拜将的遗迹，已成为汉中著名的旅游景点。《汉中府志》记载：“拜将台，在南城下，相传汉高祖拜韩信为大将，筑此以受命。今址尚存。”

During the Chu-Han Contention, Han Xin defected from Xiang Yu to Liu Bang. He hoped to be recognized and given an important position by Liu Bang. However, his expectations were not met, and he fled the Han camp in Nanzheng (now Hanzhong City). Xiao He heard about Han Xin a long time ago and believed that he was a rare talent. Fearing that a valuable asset might be lost, Xiao He pursued Han Xin without telling Liu Bang. At the foot of the Fenghuang Mountain (which is in the north of present-day Madao Town in Liuba County), Xiao He caught up with Han Xin and successfully convinced him to return. This is the story of "Xiao He pursuing Han Xin under the moonlight". After bringing Han Xin back, Xiao He recommended him to Liu Bang. He communicated that if Liu Bang wanted to be the King of Hanzhong, Han Xin might not be necessary. However, if Liu Bang intended to suppress Xiang Yu, Han Xin was a valuable ally. Liu Bang, considering Xiao He's recommendation, agreed to appoint Han Xin as a General at first. However, Xiao He suggested that Han Xin be granted the title of Commander-in-Chief and that a solemn ceremony must be held. Liu Bang accepted Xiao He's advice and chose an auspicious day for constructing a high altar and holding a grand ceremony. Han Xin was then appointed Commander-in-Chief. After the appointment, Han Xin led his troops to conquer various regions. His efforts made significant contributions to the establishment of the Han Dynasty. The present-day Baijiang Altar in Hanzhong is the remains of the altar where Han Xin was appointed Commander-in-Chief. It has become a famous tourist attraction in Hanzhong. The *Annals of Hanzhong Prefecture* recorded that the Baijiang Altar is located in the southern regions of the city to this day, and it is said that the Emperor Gaozu of Han appointed Han Xin as the Commander-in-Chief at this altar.

2.成语出处 The Source of the Idiom

（1）《汉书·高帝纪》："汉王斋戒设坛场,拜信为大将军,问以计策。"

The Book of Han: The Annals of Emperor Gao: "The emperor observed a fast, set up an altar and appointed Han Xin as his Commander-in-Chief, seeking his advice."

（2）《史记·淮阴侯列传》："王必欲拜之,择良日,斋戒,设坛场,具礼,乃可耳。""至拜大将,乃韩信也,一军皆惊。"

Records of the Grand Historian: A Biography of the Lord of Huai-yin: "If Your Majesty wishes to appoint him, choose an auspicious day, observe a fast, erect an altar, and perform rituals. Only then can it be done." "Finally, when it came to appointing a Commander-in-Chief, it was revealed to be Han Xin. The entire army was astonished."

3.成语释义 Interpreting the Idiom

筑坛拜将的意思是仰仗贤能,表示对高端人才的渴求。

This idiom signifies the importance of seeking talented individuals to depend on; it reflects the aspirations of high-caliber personnel.

4.知识拓展 Knowledge Expansion

（1）要发挥人才的重要作用，应当充分地尊重人才，而不能凭借自己的优势地位以随随便便的态度对待人才。尊重人才也需要通过一定的形式或仪式，以彰显对人才的肯定。这也有利于人才更好地发挥作用。

In order to promote the significant contributions of talented personnel, it is crucial to respect and value them. This means treating them with dignity, regardless of their position. Showing respect can be done in a specific form or via a ceremony; this not only affirms those talented person's value but also motivates them to perform at their very best.

（2）"千里马常有，而伯乐不常有。"领导者要善于发现有才能的人，善于发现别人的长处，从而实现团队价值的最大化。

"Exceptionally talented people are rare." It is the responsibility of leaders to be adept at identifying such individuals and discovering their strengths, so as to maximize team values.

第二节

Section Two

明修栈道,暗度陈仓

Mending the Plank Roads While Secretly Crossing the Chencang

1.成语故事 The Story of the Idiom

项羽封刘邦为汉王,以南郑(今汉中市)为都城。刘邦领兵入封地的途中,采纳张良的建议将沿途的栈道全部烧毁。这样既可以向项羽表示无争霸天下的心意,也可以起到阻拦追兵的作用。在南郑,刘邦养精蓄锐,等待时机以夺回关中。在进攻关中时,为了蒙骗关中守将章邯,韩信命令士兵修复栈道。章邯得知消息后,认为蜀道艰险,栈道不是那么容易修复的,即使韩信修好栈道,自己也可以轻松击溃敌军。实际上,韩信率领主力部队绕道陈仓(今宝鸡市东),从陈仓神不知鬼不觉地进入关中。章邯措手不及,仓促应战,最后战败而亡。此后,刘邦遂定三秦,并逐步统一天下,建立大汉王朝。

After Xiang Yu conferred the title of King of Han upon Liu Bang,

Liu Bang made Nanzheng (now Hanzhong City) his capital. Taking Zhang Liang's advice, Liu Bang burned down all the plank roads along the way to his fief. This gesture demonstrated his willingness to avoid competing for hegemony and also held back pursuers. In Nanzheng, Liu Bang patiently waited for an opportunity to seize Guanzhong. During the attack on Guanzhong, Han Xin ordered his soldiers to repair the plank roads in order to deceive the defender, Zhang Han. Upon hearing this news, Zhang Han believed that the roads were treacherous, and repairing the plank roads would not be an easy task. He thought that even if the roads were repaired, he could easily defeat the enemy. However, Han Xin had a different plan. He led the main forces to take a detour through Chencang (now in the east of Baoji City) and secretly entered Guanzhong. Zhang Han was caught off guard and hastily engaged in battle, resulting in his defeat and demise. Ultimately, Liu Bang decisively defeated three Qin generals, gradually unified the country, and established the Han Dynasty.

2.成语出处 The Source of the Idiom

"明修栈道，暗度陈仓"在史书中没有准确而完整的记载。《史记·淮阴侯列传》记载："八月，汉王举兵出陈仓，定三秦。"汉王刘邦通过陈仓攻入关中是有记载的，但对其是否通过明修栈道的方法来迷惑对手是没有记载的。不过在次年韩信领命攻打魏王豹的战争中，韩信使用了与"明修栈道，暗度陈仓"相同的战术倒是有记载。韩信一方面在黄河渡口故意排列战船让别人以为军队要在临晋渡河，另一方面指挥军队从夏阳渡河袭击安邑。魏王由于惊慌失措来不及抵抗而被抓获。"明修栈道，暗度陈仓"最早出现在元代的戏文中，表达对韩信用兵的崇敬之情。

This idiom lacks accurate historical records. It's mentioned in *Re-*

cords of the Grand Historian: A Biography of the Lord of Huaiyin: "In August, the King of Han led the army via Chencang and took control of the Guanzhong area." This historical record confirms Liu Bang's seizure of Guanzhong via Chencang, but it doesn't mention the tactic of confusing his opponents by mending the plank roads. However, during the following year's war, when Han Xin was ordered to attack Bao, the King of Wei, there is a documented instance of Han Xin employing this kind of tactic. Han Xin strategically placed boats at the Yellow River Ferry in Linjin to deceive others into thinking that his troops would cross the river there, while he actually crossed from Xiayang and launched an attack on Anyi. The panicked King of Wei was captured without resistance. The idiom "mending the plank roads while secretly crossing the Chencang" first appeared in the Yuan Dynasty drama scripts to honor Han Xin's military prowess.

3.成语释义 Interpreting the Idiom

"明修栈道，暗度陈仓"是指将真实的意图隐藏在表面的行动背后，用明显的行动迷惑对方，使对方产生错觉并忽略行动背后的真实意图，从而出奇制胜；比喻用假象迷惑对方以达到其他目的。

栈道是指在悬崖峭壁的险要地方凿孔支架、铺上木板而建成的通道，可供行军、运输粮草辎重，也可供马帮商旅通行。在古代，由关中通往汉中和蜀地的悬崖上常常建有栈道。在现在汉中的褒河镇，还能够看到仿古修建的褒斜栈道。

This idiom refers to the strategy of concealing one's true intentions behind apparent actions, confusing the opponents with overt actions, creating an illusion that diverts their attention from one's true intentions of actions, and ultimately achieving victory through unexpected means. It metaphorically signifies the use of deception or illusion to achieve

alternative objectives.

The term "plank road" refers to a pathway constructed by drilling holes and laying planks on precarious cliffs. It served as a means for military marches, transportation of supplies, and the passage of caravans and travelers. In ancient times, when people wanted to travel from Guanzhong to Hanzhong and Shu region, the construction of plank roads along cliff edges was often necessary for safe passage. In present-day Baohe Town of Hanzhong, one can still observe the reconstructed Bao-Xie Plank Road, which replicates the ancient design.

4.知识拓展 Knowledge Expansion

以奇用兵一直是中国推崇的用兵方略。"明修栈道，暗度陈仓"正是在具体军事战斗中使用的以奇用兵的典型代表。与其同义的还有出奇制胜、声东击西等成语。

The use of unconventional tactics has long been revered in Chinese military strategy. The idiom "mending the plank roads while secretly crossing the Chencang" serves as a prime example of employing such tactics in specific military engagements. It is synonymous with other idioms such as "winning by surprise" and "making a diversionary attack to the east while attacking to the west".

韩信将兵，多多益善

Han Xin Leading the Troops: The More, The Better

1.成语故事 The Story of the Idiom

汉高祖刘邦有一次坦然地和韩信讨论将军们的高下，认为他们各有所长，各有不足。刘邦问韩信："以我这样的才能能率领多少军队？"韩信说："陛下只能率领十万军队。"刘邦又问："那你呢？"韩信回答："我是兵马越多越好。"刘邦笑着说："你说越多越好，那为什么还被我俘虏了？"韩信说："陛下不善于带兵，却善于任用将领。这就是我被陛下俘虏的原因。何况陛下的才能是上天赐予的，不是普通人能拥有的。"

Emperor Liu Bang, the founder of the Han Dynasty, once had a candid discussion with Han Xin about the strengths and weaknesses of his generals. Liu Bang asked Han Xin, "How many troops do you think I am capable of leading?" Han Xin replied, "Your Majesty, you can command an army of up to a hundred thousand soldiers." Liu Bang then asked, "And what about yourself?" Han Xin answered, "The more soldiers, the better." Liu Bang chuckled and inquired, "Then why was I able to capture you?" Han Xin explained, "Your Majesty, your strength lies in selecting and utilizing talented generals, rather than personally leading soldiers. That is why I was captured by you. Moreover, Your Majesty's exceptional abilities are a divine gift, surpassing those of ordinary individuals."

2.成语出处 The Source of the Idiom

《史记·淮阴侯列传》:"上常从容与信言诸将能不,各有差。上问曰:'如我能将几何? '信曰:'陛下不过能将十万。'上曰:'于君何如? '曰:'臣多多而益善耳。'上笑曰:'多多益善,何为我禽? '信曰:'陛下不能将兵,而善将将,此乃信之所以为陛下禽也。且陛下所谓天授,非人力也。'"

Records of the Grand Historian: A Biography of the Lord of Huaiyin: "Emperor Liu Bang, the founder of the Han Dynasty, once had a candid discussion with Han Xin about the strengths and weaknesses of his generals. Liu Bang asked Han Xin, 'How many troops do you think I am capable of leading?' Han Xin replied, 'Your Majesty, you can command an army of up to a hundred thousand soldiers.' Liu Bang then asked, 'And what about yourself?' Han Xin answered, 'The more soldiers, the better.' Liu Bang chuckled and inquired, 'Then why was I able to capture you?' Han Xin explained, 'Your Majesty, your strength lies in selecting and utilizing talented generals, rather than personally leading soldiers. That is why I was captured by you. Moreover, Your Majesty's exceptional abilities are a divine gift, surpassing those of ordinary individuals.'"

3.成语释义 Interpreting the Idiom

　　韩信最初投奔项羽,没有得到重用,就转而投奔刘邦,经丞相萧何极力推荐,才担任汉军的大将军。韩信施展自己的军事才能,为汉王朝的建立立下了汗马功劳,被封为齐王。一次刘邦与韩信讨论各自率军的能力时,问韩信能够带多少兵。韩信说自己领军打仗,带领的军队是越多越好。"韩信将兵,多多益善"比喻越多越好,一般用于表示对事物的需求量大,而且质量可以不受限制。

　　Han Xin initially sought refuge with Xiang Yu, but he did not receive significant recognition. He subsequently defected from Xiang Yu and turned to Liu Bang. With the strong recommendation of Prime Minister Xiao He, Liu Bang appointed Han Xin as the Commander-in-Chief. Han Xin showcased his military talent and made significant contributions to the establishment of the Han Dynasty, earning the title of the King of Qi. During a discussion between Liu Bang and Han Xin about their respective abilities to lead troops, Liu Bang inquired about the number of soldiers Han Xin was capable of commanding. Han Xin replied that the more soldiers he led in battle, the better. This idiom, "Han Xin leading the troops: the more, the better", emphasizes a preference for greater quantity. It is commonly used to describe situations where there is a high demand for something, and the quality is unrestricted.

4.知识拓展 Knowledge Expansion

　　与多多益善意思相反的是宁缺毋滥。宁缺毋滥表示宁愿空缺,也不要降低标准,一味求多。

　　An antonymous idiom of "the more, the better" is "better to be

lacking than excessive". This saying conveys the notion that it is preferable to have a scarcity rather than compromising standards and blindly pursuing quantity.

5.成语启示 Further Insight

这个故事告诉我们,刘邦善于统领众将,而韩信善于带兵,说明人各有所长,各有所短。因此,我们要扬长避短,发挥自己的优势。

In the story, Liu Bang demonstrates exceptional command ability over his generals, while Han Xin excels at leading troops. It serves as a reminder that each individual possesses his/her own strengths and weaknesses. As a result, it is important for us to leverage our strengths and mitigate our weaknesses.

第四节

Section Four

———

运筹帷幄

Strategize from Behind the Curtains

1.成语故事 The Story of the Idiom

　　西汉初年，天下已定，汉高祖刘邦在雒阳（今河南省洛阳市）南宫摆设酒席。刘邦问分封的诸侯和将领他得到天下和项羽失去天下的原因。有人回答说是刘邦能够与大家共享利益，而项羽嫉贤妒能，不能论功行赏。刘邦对此并不认同，认为原因在于自己能够正确任用人才，充分发挥他们的作用，做到人尽其才，并对张良、萧何、韩信进行了点评。他认为张良能够在帷帐中运筹决策，决胜于千里之外，在这方面自己不如张良；在镇守国家、安抚百姓、畅通粮道等方面自己不如萧何；在率领大军攻城拔寨方面自己不如韩信。

In the early years of the Western Han Dynasty, with the country already stabilized, Emperor Liu Bang hosted a banquet in the South Palace of Luoyang (now in Luoyang City, Henan Province). During the banquet, Liu Bang asked his vassals and generals about the reasons behind his successful conquest of the empire while Xiang Yu had failed. Some attendees responded that Liu Bang's success was attributed to his willingness to share the spoils with everyone, contrasting with Xiang Yu's envy of talents and failure to reward people based on merits. However, Liu Bang disagreed with this viewpoint. He believed that his success lay in his ability to select the right people and fully utilize their talents, allowing each individual to reach his/her full potential.Liu Bang then proceeded to provide his assessments of Zhang Liang, Xiao He, and Han Xin. He acknowledged Zhang Liang's strategic prowess in making decisions within his tent and accurately predicting the outcome of battles taking place thousands of miles away. Regarding Xiao He, Liu Bang recognized his superior skills in defending the country, pacifying the people, and ensuring the smooth transportation of food supplies. Liu Bang also acknowledged Han Xin's exceptional military ability in leading the army to successfully besiege cities and conquer enemy strongholds. Liu Bang admitted that he fell short of those abilities compared to them.

2.成语出处 The Source of the Idiom

（1）《史记·高祖本纪》："高祖曰：'夫运筹策帷帐之中，决胜于千里之外，吾不如子房。'"

Records of the Grand Historian: A Biography of the Emperor Gaozu: "Emperor Gaozu states: 'Zifang surpasses me in strategizing, effortlessly foreseeing remote battles with precise decisions made from his command post.'"

（2）《史记·留侯世家》："高祖曰：'运筹策帷帐中，决胜千里外，子房功也。'"

Records of the Grand Historian: A Biography of the Lord of Liu: "Emperor Gaozu states: 'Zifang's wisdom and skills are credited for the success of those strategic choices.'"

3.成语释义 Interpreting the Idiom

运筹帷幄指在军帐内谋划、指挥，后泛指在后方制订作战方案，也泛指主持大计、考虑决策。帷幄指古代军中帐幕。

The idiom refers to planning and commanding from within a military tent. It originally meant devising operational plans from a rear position, but it has since come to signify taking charge of major plans and significant decisions. The word "curtains" in this idiom refers to the military tent in ancient times.

4.知识拓展 Knowledge Expansion

（1）张良，字子房，是刘邦的重要谋士，与韩信、萧何并称"汉初三杰"。张良虽然不曾独立带兵打仗，不曾立下战功，但是因擅于出谋划策而为刘邦所倚重，被册封为留侯。张良因其足智多谋且功成不居的品格而为后世敬仰。汉中留坝县留侯镇建的庙宇奉祠，因张良曾被册封为留侯，故名"留侯祠"，俗称"张良庙"，是当地祭拜张良的重要场所，也是当地重要的旅游景点。

Zhang Liang, also known by his courtesy name Zifang, was a crucial strategist and counselor to Liu Bang. Together with Han Xin and Xiao He, they were recognized as the "Three Outstanding Heroes of the Early Han Dynasty". Although Zhang Liang never personally led troops or achieved military merits, he excelled in offering strategic advice and gained Liu Bang's trust, leading to his appointment as a Marquis. Zhang Liang's remarkable resourcefulness and humility in claiming no credit for his service have earned him admiration from later generations. In present-day Liuba County, Hanzhong City, there stands a memorial temple known as the Marquis of Liu Temple, dedicated to Zhang Liang. The temple's name originates from Zhang Liang's bestowed title and serves as a significant destination for local worship and an important attraction for tourists in the area.

（2）运筹帷幄的同义词有足智多谋、出谋划策、指挥若定。

Its synonyms include "being full of resources", "giving counsel", and "commanding as if victory is assured".

第五节
Section Five

萧规曹随

Follow the Established Rules

1.成语故事 The Story of the Idiom

萧何是西汉开国功臣之一,任职相国期间,根据民众痛恨秦朝苛法的情况,顺应历史潮流除旧更新,奉行道家学说,推行休养生息的政策。萧何病重时向汉惠帝举荐了曹参,让他接替自己的职位。早年曹参与萧何交好,但等到各自建功立业之后反倒生了嫌隙。萧何病故后,汉惠帝依萧何生前举荐以及曹参在任齐国相国期间的政绩而封曹参为相。曹参任丞相之后,做事没有任何变更,一概遵循萧何制定的法规制度。对此,大臣甚至皇帝都有些疑惑,曹参对皇帝解释说:"高祖平定了天下,法令已经明确并且富有成效,我们遵循原有的法令而不需要随意变更。"曹参做相国期间,极力主张清静无为,给了百姓休养生息的机会,因此得到百姓的称颂。《史记·曹相国世家》中也有记载,"百姓歌之曰:萧何为法,讲若画一;曹参代之,守而勿失。载其清净,民以宁一。"其意为:萧何制定法令,明确划一;曹参接替萧何为相,遵守萧何制定的法度不变。曹参施行清静无为的做法，百姓因而安宁不乱。

Xiao He was one of the founding heroes of the Western Han Dynasty. As Prime Minister, he responded to public discontents with the harsh laws of the Qin Dynasty by embracing the prevailing historical trend of reform. He implemented policies inspired by Taoism to promote recuperation and rejuvenation. When Xiao He fell seriously ill, he recommended Cao Shen to Emperor Hui as his successor. Cao Shen and Xiao He had been on good terms in their early years, but as they both achieved success, their relationship deteriorated and grievances arose. After Xiao He died, Emperor Hui honored Xiao He's recommendation and appointed Cao Shen Prime Minister based on his governing achievements while serving as the Prime Minister of Qi. Once assuming the role, Cao Shen followed the existing laws and regulations established by Xiao He without making any changes. This puzzled both the ministers and the emperor. Cao Shen explained that since Emperor Gaozu had already brought stability to the empire, the laws and decrees he and his ministers made were proven effective. Therefore, there was no need for arbitrary modifications. During his tenure as Prime Minister, Cao Shen advocated for a policy highlighting the importance of rest, providing the people with an opportunity to recover. As a result, he received acclaim from the populace. *Records of the Grand Historian: A Biography of the Prime Minister Cao* chronicles the story of how the Han Dynasty Prime Minister, Cao Shen, followed the rules set by his predecessor, Xiao He.

2.成语出处 The Source of the Idiom

《史记·曹相国世家》:"参代何为汉相国,举事无所变更,一遵萧何约束。"

Records of the Grand Historian: A Biography of the Prime Minister Cao: "Cao Shen took over as the premier in place of Xiao He, and the governing approaches remained unaltered, simply adhering to the guidelines and protocols established by Xiao He."

3.成语释义 Interpreting the Idiom

萧规曹随的意思是曹参做了宰相后仍实行萧何之前制定的规章制度,比喻按照前人的成规办事。

This idiom means that after Cao Shen became the Prime Minister, he continued to implement the rules and regulations established by his predecessor, Xiao He. It metaphorically signifies following the established practices of predecessors.

4.知识拓展 Knowledge Expansion

萧规曹随最早是褒义词,指按照规矩办事;后来逐渐演变为贬义词,比喻不知变通,生搬硬套,与因循守旧、故步自封、墨守成规等成语意思相近。

Originally, this idiom had a positive connotation, referring to the act of adhering to rules and regulations. However, as time went on, it gradually acquired a negative connotation, signifying an inability to adapt, rigid adherence, and blind conformity. It is synonymous with expressions such as conservatism, complacency, and conformity.

5.成语启示 Further Insight

（1）萧规曹随可当作褒义词理解和使用。在客观条件没有根本性改变的情况下，之前有效的政策、方针或者战略依然是可行的，就不能随意变更，更不能为了改变而改变，不能随意另起炉灶。

This idiom should be interpreted and employed in a commendatory sense. When objective conditions remain fundamentally unchanged, the effective policies, principles, or strategies that have been previously established continue to be viable. Therefore, they should not be altered haphazardly or for the sake of change alone. It is important to avoid abandoning them and starting anew without valid reasons.

（2）萧规曹随是一个富有智慧的政治策略，也是关于执行力的经典案例。我们应当保持战略定力，在确定目标之后，不动摇、不松懈，为了实现目标而持续努力，不断奋斗。

The approach is a wise strategy that exemplifies effective execution. It emphasizes the importance of strategic resilience. Once we have determined our goals, we should remain steadfast, unwavering, and persistent in our efforts to achieve them. We must continue to exert ourselves and strive towards our objectives without faltering.

三国成语典故悦读

Enchanting Tales of Idioms from the Three Kingdoms

第一节
Section One

如鱼得水

Like a Fish Finding Water

1. 成语故事 The Story of the Idiom

刘备投靠荆州牧刘表之后,奉命驻扎在新野。可刘备是个胸怀大志的人,他并不想长久寄人篱下,就四处搜罗人才为己所用。这个时候徐庶向他隆重推荐诸葛亮,认为诸葛亮是真正的人才,建议刘备亲自登门拜会。刘备求贤若渴,三次亲自到诸葛亮居住的茅庐(今襄阳市古隆中)去拜访。诸葛亮看到刘备非常诚恳,第三次才同意与刘备见面。刘备向他请教治理国家的方法,诸葛亮仔细分析了当时的局势,向刘备提出了三分天下的建议——占据荆州和益州,形成与曹操、孙权对立之势,进而争夺天下以成霸业。刘备听后非常赞同诸葛亮的对策,后来他和诸葛亮的关系逐渐密切,感情也不断加深。关羽和张飞等人对此不解,还在私底下议论。刘备知道后对二人说:"我有了诸葛亮,就像鱼儿遇到水一样。你们就不要再随便议论了。"

After Liu Bei sought refuge with Liu Biao, the Imperial Protector of Jingzhou, he was stationed in Xinye. Liu Bei, a man with grand ambitions, did not wish to rely on others for long. He actively searched for talented individuals to join his cause. During this time, Xu Shu highly recommended Zhuge Liang, regarding him as a true talent, and suggested Liu Bei meet him in person. Driven by his thirst for capable individuals, Liu Bei made three personal visits to the thatched cottage where Zhuge Liang resided (now known as Gulongzhong in Xiangyang). Zhuge Liang recognized Liu's sincere determination and finally agreed to a meeting at Liu's third visit. Liu Bei sought Zhuge Liang's counsel on governing the country, and Zhuge Liang carefully analyzed the current situation. He proposed a strategy to divide the realm into three parts: occupying Jingzhou and Yizhou, establishing a tripartite balance of power with Cao Cao and Sun Quan, and then competing for dominance to achieve greatness. Liu Bei wholeheartedly embraced Zhuge Liang's strategy, and their relationship gradually grew closer, deepening their bond. Guan Yu, Zhang Fei, and others couldn't understand this and privately expressed their discontents. Upon learning of their dissatisfaction, Liu Bei said to them, "With Zhuge Liang by my side, it is like a fish finding water. You should refrain from such casual discussions."

2. 成语出处 The Source of the Idiom

《三国志·蜀书·诸葛亮传》："关羽、张飞等不悦，先主解之曰：'孤之有孔明，犹鱼之有水也。愿诸君勿复言。'"

The Records of the Three Kingdoms—The Book of Shu: A Biogra-

phy of Zhuge Liang: "When Guan Yu, Zhang Fei, and others expressed their displeasure, Liu Bei reassured them, saying, 'Having Zhuge Liang by my side is like a fish finding water. Please refrain from raising such concerns.'"

3. 成语释义 Interpreting the Idiom

如鱼得水的意思就是好像鱼得到水一样,比喻遇到跟自己投合的人,或进入适合自己的环境。其近义词有如虎添翼、情投意合等。

This idiom metaphorically signifies that someone meets a person who is very compatible with oneself or sets foot in an environment that is highly suitable. Synonyms for this idiom are "like a tiger with added wings", "perfect match of emotions and intentions", and so on.

4. 知识拓展 Knowledge Expansion

刘备与诸葛亮之间的鱼水关系受到后世的仰慕,有诗人对其做了饱含深情的描绘。例如:"鱼水从相得,山河遂有归"(出自唐代李中的《读蜀志》)以及"出身感三顾,鱼水相后先"(出自宋代曾巩的《隆中》)。还有诗人通过对鱼与水和谐关系的描绘,表达对自然和谐之美的赞赏。例如:"西塞山前白鹭飞,桃花流水鳜鱼肥"(出自唐代张志和的《渔歌子·西塞山前白鹭飞》)以及"生成泽广时芳茂,鱼水情通乐韵谐"(出自唐代徐铉的《应制赏花》)。

The close relationship between Liu Bei and Zhuge Liang is revered by future generations, with poets in ancient times depicting it affectionately in their poems. For example, "Fish and water naturally find harmony; mountains and rivers thus have their place to return" (from "Reading the Records of Shu" by Li Zhong, the Tang Dynasty), and

027

"Arising from the depths, I feel the echoes of three calls; like fish and water, in succession we follow one after the other" (from "Longzhong" by Zenggong, the Song Dynasty). In ancient poetry, the depiction of the harmonious relationship between fish and water reflects an appreciation for the beauty of harmony in nature. Examples include, "In front of Xisai Mountain, white egrets fly, with peach blossoms by the water and fat mandarin fish in the stream" (from "Fisherman's Song at Sea: Egrets Flying Before Xisai Mountain" by Zhang Zhihe, the Tang Dynasty), and "When the marshlands are vast, fragrant plants flourish; fish and water share a bond, harmonizing in joyous tune" (from "In Response to an Imperial Order: Appreciating Flowers" by Xu Xuan, the Tang Dynasty).

第二节
Section Two

对酒当歌

The Ballad of the Short-Song

1. 成语故事 The Story of the Idiom

建安十三年(公元 208 年)冬,曹操亲率大军列阵长江,与"孙刘联盟"对垒于赤壁,意欲收复江南,一统天下。在此之前,曹操已经先后击败吕布、袁术等豪强集团,又在官渡之战一举消灭了强大的袁绍势力,并征服乌桓,统一了北方,轻而易举地拿下了荆州。一天夜晚,月光皎洁,曹操在大江之上置酒设乐,宴请诸将,酒酣畅怀,横槊而歌,吟诵了"对酒当歌,人生几何"的千古绝唱,即《短歌行》。曹操一直强调"唯才是举",他的《短歌行》实际上也是一首"求贤曲"。它运用了诗歌的形式,蕴含着丰富的情感,抒发了曹操求贤若渴的迫切心情。

In the winter of the thirteenth year of the Jian'an era (208 AD), Cao Cao led his massive army to confront the Sun-Liu Alliance at Chibi.

He intended to assert control over the southern region and then achieve the unification of the nation. Cao Cao had already defeated formidable adversaries such as Lü Bu and Yuan Shu. He had also secured a decisive victory against Yuan Shao in the Battle of Guandu, conquered the Wuhuan tribe, unified the northern territories, and effortlessly captured Jingzhou. One night, under the bright moonlight, Cao Cao hosted a grand feast on the river. With wine cups raised high, he reveled in the company of his esteemed generals. In his exuberance, he composed and sang the timeless masterpiece, known as "The Ballad of the Short-Song", with these opening lines "Before wine, sing a song; How long is life, how long?" Throughout his career, Cao Cao consistently stressed the significance of nurturing and promoting talented individuals. The "Ballad of the Short-Song" serves as a hymn that celebrates such exceptional abilities. Through the artistry of poetry, this composition conveys profound emotions and reflects Cao Cao's ardent desire for capable individuals.

2. 成语出处 The Source of the Idiom

曹操所赋的诗歌《短歌行》。

This idiom originates from a poem called "The Ballad of the Short-Song" composed by Cao Cao.

3. 成语释义 Interpreting the Idiom

对酒当歌的意思是人生时间有限,应该有所作为;后来也指及时行乐。

This idiom originally conveys the meaning that life is limited, and one should strive to accomplish something within that time. However, it later is also used to express the idea of seizing the moment to indulge in pleasure and enjoyment.

4. 知识拓展 Knowledge Expansion

短歌行

曹　操

对酒当歌,人生几何!

譬如朝露,去日苦多。

慨当以慷,忧思难忘。

何以解忧? 唯有杜康。

青青子衿,悠悠我心。

但为君故,沉吟至今。

呦呦鹿鸣,食野之苹。

我有嘉宾,鼓瑟吹笙。

明明如月,何时可掇?

忧从中来,不可断绝。

越陌度阡,枉用相存。

契阔谈讌,心念旧恩。

月明星稀,乌鹊南飞。

绕树三匝,何枝可依?

山不厌高,海不厌深。

周公吐哺,天下归心。

The Ballad of the Short-Song

Cao Cao

Before wine, sing a song;

How long is life, how long?

It seems like morning dew

With bygones gone with woe.

O sing loud and sing free,

And yet my cause frets me.

What can kill sorrow mine?

Nothing but Dukang Wine.

Blue, blue the scholar gown

Seek, seek I up and down.

In your esteem I bow

And have chanted till now.

The deer each to each bleat;

Afield they wormwood eat.

I have good guests today;

The lute and flute we play.

Fair, fair the moon does shine;

Could I have it? I pine!

My heart's laden with care,

Which seems to stay for e'er.

Through the field lies the lane;

It's for you, not in vain.

We talk throughout repast;

Remembe'ring your grace past.

The moon's bright and stars few;

Fly south magpie and crow.

Thrice they go round the birch,

But on which bough to perch?

Let mounts be high and steep

And the seas broad and deep.

O our sage Prince of Chough,

To your side all would go.

（赵彦春[1]翻译）

---

1 赵彦春.翻译诗学散论[M].青岛:青岛出版社,2007 年.

第三节

Section Three

———

将计就计

Beating Someone at Their Own Game

1. 成语故事 The Story of the Idiom

赤壁大战前夕,曹操亲率大军驻扎在长江北岸,意欲横渡长江直下东吴。东吴都督周瑜也带兵与曹军隔江对峙,双方剑拔弩张。蒋干是曹操手下的谋士,因曾与周瑜同窗数载,便在曹操面前毛遂自荐,要过江到东吴去做说客,劝降周瑜。周瑜闻讯就猜出蒋干来意,于是摆下"群英会",诱导他盗走假的曹军水师都督蔡瑁、张允二人的"投降书"。周瑜知道曹军中只有蔡、张二将精通水战,而且曹操疑心很重,便设下此计,想借曹操之手杀掉他们。曹操果真上了当,斩了蔡瑁、张允。等到曹操明白过来为时已晚,只好另换了两个水军都督。结果,赤壁一战,曹军一败涂地。这就是蒋干盗书——一个将计就计的故事。

Before the Battle of Chibi, Cao Cao led a massive army stationed on the north bank of the Changjiang River, intending to cross the river and advance toward Kingdom of Wu. Zhou Yu, Commander-in-Chief of the Wu army, led his troops to confront the Cao army from across the river, and escalating tensions between the two sides mounted. Jiang Gan, a strategist under Cao's command and childhood friend of Zhou Yu, volunteered to act as an intermediary and persuade Zhou to surrender. Anticipating Jiang Gan's intentions, Zhou arranged a "Meeting of Heroes" and deceived Jiang Gan into stealing a fabricated "Letter of Surrender" purportedly written by Cao's loyal naval commanders, Cai Mao and Zhang Yun. Recognizing that only Cai Mao and Zhang Yun possessed expertise in naval warfare within Cao's army and Cao was suspicious, Zhou devised this plan to manipulate Cao into eliminating them. Falling into the trap, Cao executed Cai Mao and Zhang Yun. However, it was too late when Cao realized his mistake, and he had to appoint two new naval commanders. The subsequent Battle of Chibi resulted in a resounding defeat for Cao's army. This story recounts Jiang Gan's theft of the fabricated letter and serves as a tale of beating someone at their own game.

2. 成语出处 The Source of the Idiom

罗贯中著的《三国演义》第四十五回 "三江口曹操折兵，群英会蒋干中计"。

This idiom is from Chapter 45 of *Romance of the Three Kingdoms* by Luo Guanzhong, titled "At Sanjiangkou, Cao Cao Loses Soldiers; In The Meeting Of Heroes, Jiang Gan Is Lured Into A Ruse".

3. 成语释义 Interpreting the Idiom

将计就计的意思是利用对方的计策,反过来向对方施计。与其有相似意思的有"以其人之道,还治其人之身"。

This idiom means to utilize the opponent's strategies against them. A synonymous phrase of this idiom is "fight fire with fire".

4. 知识拓展 Knowledge Expansion

将计就计是一个脍炙人口的成语,与其相关的事例也经常发生。据说明朝末年,皇太极举兵进犯中原,遭到了袁崇焕的英勇阻拦。皇太极正愁没机会突破袁崇焕这一关时,恰巧手下人抓了两个皇宫里的太监,皇太极便想起蒋干盗书的故事。于是他安排一个将军当"周瑜",和这两个太监同住,半夜里故意和别人讲袁崇焕和皇太极有密谋。一个太监装睡,就做了偷听的"蒋干",然后逃回京城向崇祯皇帝报告。崇祯皇帝由于猜忌心重,就把袁崇焕召回京城,以谋反罪将其处死。这也是典型的"将计就计"的故事。

The idiom "beating someone at their own game" is a widely known saying that is often exemplified in similar instances. It is said that during the late Ming Dynasty, when Huang Taiji led his troops to invade the Central Plains but was resisted by the brave general Yuan Chonghuan and his soldiers. When Huang Taiji was concerned about breaking through Yuan's defense, his subordinates captured two eunuchs. This reminded him of the story of Jiang Gan stealing the fabricated letter. He then arranged for a general to play the role of "Zhou Yu" and live together with the captured eunuchs. In the middle of the night, the general deliberately discussed Yuan Chonghuan's "conspiracy" with Huang Taiji in front of others, while one eunuch, pretending to be asleep, acted as the eavesdropping "Jiang Gan". Afterwards, the eunuch effortlessly escaped back to the capital to report to Emperor Chongzhen. Due to his excessive suspicion, Emperor Chongzhen summoned Yuan Chonghuan to the capital city and executed him for treason. This is yet another typical story of "beating someone at their own game".

第四节

Section Four

———

反客为主

The Interchange of Host and Guest

1. 成语故事 The Story of the Idiom

　　三国时期,刘备统率大军攻打汉中。汉中的守将夏侯渊得到消息后,马上向曹操汇报;曹操下令应战,并亲自率四十万大军随后支援。两军在汉中定军山展开了激战。先是曹军夏侯渊一方生擒了黄忠一方的大将陈式。黄忠连忙去和谋士法正商量。法正建议说:"夏侯渊性格轻浮急躁,做事有勇无谋。我们可以激励自己的士兵,每前进一步就设下一道营垒,引诱夏侯渊来交战,然后再擒获他。这就是所谓的'反客为主'的计策。"黄忠采纳了法正的建议,先把自己的所有物品都奖励给士兵以鼓舞士气。士兵们非常高兴,都愿意拼死作战,然后每前进一步都设下一道营垒,并在每道营垒里住几天,巩固住阵地再往前推进。夏侯渊听说后打算出战,他的属下张郃识出这是"反客为主"之计,劝他不可出战,假如出战就会失败。夏侯渊不听,命令夏侯尚带领几千名士兵出战,一直冲到了黄忠的营寨前。黄忠提刀与夏侯尚交战,只一个回合便活捉了夏侯尚。曹军大败。

During the Three Kingdoms Period, Liu Bei led a formidable army to attack Hanzhong. Upon receiving this news, Xiahou Yuan, the defender of Hanzhong, promptly reported it to Cao Cao. Cao ordered a counterattack and personally led a 400,000-strong army to provide reinforcement. The two armies were engaged in intense warfare at Dingjun Mountain in Hanzhong. Initially, Xiahou Yuan's forces captured Chen Shi, a general serving under Huang Zhong. In response, Huang Zhong sought the counsel of his strategist, Fa Zheng. Fa Zheng proposed a plan, saying, "Xiahou Yuan is impulsive and lacks strategic acumen. We can motivate our soldiers to construct new camps after every forward movement, luring Xiahou Yuan into battle, and then capture him. This strategy is known as the 'Ruse of the Interchange of Host and Guest'." Huang Zhong accepted Fa Zheng's advice and rewarded his soldiers with his own belongings to inspire them and uplift their morale. The soldiers were delighted and willing to fight bravely. They advanced methodically, establishing camps at each stage to solidify their position before advancing farther. When Xiahou Yuan learned of their actions, he intended to engage in battle. However, his subordinate Zhang He discerned their actions as a ploy of "turning a guest into a host" and advised against battle, warning of the inevitable defeat. Disregarding the advice, Xiahou Yuan ordered Xiahou Shang to lead several thousand soldiers in a charge towards Huang Zhong's camp. Huang Zhong confronted Xiahou Shang with his sword, and within a single encounter, captured Xiahou Shang alive. Cao Cao's army suffered a major defeat.

2. 成语出处 The Source of the Idiom

罗贯中著的《三国演义》第七十一回"占对山黄忠逸待劳,据汉水赵云寡胜众":"忠慌与法正商议,正曰:'渊为人轻躁,恃勇少谋。可激劝士卒,拔寨前进,步步为营,诱渊来战而擒之。此乃"反客为主"之法。'"

This idiom is from Chapter 71 of *Romance of the Three Kingdoms* by Luo Guanzhong, titled "At the Capture of Opposite Hill, Huang Zhong Scores A Success; On the River Han, Zhao Yun Conquers A Host": "Huang Zhong at once asked advice from Fa Zheng, who said, 'This Xiahou Yuan is easily provoked to anger, and being angry he is bold without discretion. Now is to work up the enthusiasm of our soldiers, then break camps and advance. Do this in a series of marches, and we will excite him up to the point of giving battle, then we can capture him. They call this the "Ruse of the Interchange of Host and Guest".'"

3. 成语释义 Interpreting the Idiom

反客为主的字面意思是客人反过来成为主人,比喻变被动为主动。与其意思相近的成语有鸠占鹊巢、喧宾夺主、主客颠倒。

This idiom has a literal meaning of shifting roles from being a guest to becoming a host. Metaphorically, it signifies a transition from a passive position to an active one. Synonyms of this idiom include "the turtledove occupying the magpie's nest", "usurping the host's role", and "the reversal of roles between the host and the guest".

4. 知识拓展 Knowledge Expansion

(1)三十六计之反客为主:"乘隙插足,扼其主机,渐之进也。"

One of the Thirty-Six Stratagems known as the "Ruse of the Interchange of Host and Guest": "Usurp leadership in a situation where you are normally subordinate. Infiltrate your target by initially pretending to be a guest seeking acceptance, but gradually assert control from within and eventually become the owner."

（2）定军山，位于今陕西省汉中市勉县城南，曾是三国时期战场，时人称"得定军山则得汉中，得汉中则定天下"，以三国时蜀汉大将黄忠于汉中之战斩杀曹魏大将夏侯渊闻名；现为省级风景名胜区。

Dingjun Mountain is located at the south of Mianxian County in Hanzhong City, Shaanxi Province. It was a historical site of the Three Kingdoms Periods, and was widely known for the saying, "If you secure Dingjun Mountain, you secure Hanzhong; if you secure Hanzhong, you secure the world".This saying stems from the momentous Battle of Hanzhong, where Huang Zhong, a renowned general of the Shu Kingdom, successfully defeated Xiahou Yuan, a prominent general of the Wei Kingdom. Today, Dingjun Mountain is designated as a provincial-level scenic area.

第五节

Section Five
————

偃旗息鼓

Lower the Banners and Silence the Drums

1. 成语故事 The Story of the Idiom

　　在争夺汉中的一次战斗中,蜀将黄忠杀死了曹将夏侯渊,并夺取了战略要地。曹操非常恼火,亲率大军向阳平关进攻。黄忠得到趁夜烧劫曹军粮草的任务。他临行前和赵云约定了返回时间,过期不归赵云就带兵出寨接应。赵云带兵侦察时与曹操亲自统率的部队相遇,便同曹军厮杀起来,把曹军打得丢盔弃甲,救回了黄忠。曹操没有善罢甘休,指挥大队人马一路追杀赵云,直扑蜀营。赵云的副将张翼见赵云已回本寨,后面追兵来势凶猛,便要关闭寨门。赵云却下令打开寨门,偃旗息鼓,准备放曹军进来;又命令弓弩手埋伏在寨内外,然后自己单枪匹马站在门口等候敌人。生性多疑的曹操追到寨门口,心想寨门大开,必有伏兵,立即下令撤退。就在曹操调头后退的时候,蜀军营里金鼓齐鸣,杀声震天,飞箭如雨般射向曹军。曹军惊慌失措,夺路逃命,自相践踏。赵云趁势夺了曹军的粮草,杀了曹军大批兵马,得胜回营。

During the battle for control of Hanzhong, Huang Zhong, a general of the Shu Kingdom, killed Xiahou Yuan, one of Cao Cao's generals, and captured a strategic location. Enraged, Cao Cao personally led a large army to launch a major attack on Yangping Pass. Huang Zhong was ordered to set fire to Cao Cao's grain depot at night. Before his departure, Huang Zhong made an agreement with Zhao Yun that if he did not return within a specified time, Zhao Yun should lead troops to provide assistance. When Zhao Yun ventured out of the camp to rescue Huang, he encountered Cao's army. Engaging in fierce combat, Zhao Yun defeated the enemy forces and successfully brought Huang Zhong back to the camp. However, Cao Cao was relentless and ordered his troops to pursue Zhao Yun, heading straight to the Shu camp. Zhang Yi, Zhao Yun's deputy, observed Zhao Yun's return to the camp, but noticed the pursuing enemy forces were formidable. He suggested closing the gate and defending the camp. Contrary to Zhang Yi's suggestion, Zhao Yun commanded that the gate should remain wide open, the banners to be lowered, and the drums to be silenced, creating an illusion of calmness. He strategically positioned archers both inside and outside the camp, while he himself stood alone at the gate, awaiting the enemy's arrival. Cao Cao, ever suspicious, reached the gate, suspecting an ambush, and hastily ordered a retreat. Just as Cao Cao's forces were withdrawing, the sound of drums reverberated throughout the Shu camp, and a deluge of arrows rained towards Cao Cao's army. The panicked soldiers trampled one another in a desperate attempt to escape. Seizing the opportunity, Zhao Yun captured Cao Cao's provisions, inflicted heavy casualties upon Cao's troops, and emerged victorious from the battle.

2. 成语出处 The Source of the Idiom

《三国志·蜀书·赵云传》,裴松之注引《赵云别传》:"云入营,更大开门,偃旗息鼓。公军疑云有伏兵,引去。"

The Records of the Three Kingdoms —The Book of Shu: A Biography of Zhao Yun, Pei Songzhi cited the "Unofficial Biography of Zhao Yun" when he wrote: "When Zhao Yun entered the camp, he opened the gates even wider, lowered the flags, and silenced the drums. The enemy army suspected that Zhao Yun set an ambush, so they withdrew."

3. 成语释义 Interpreting the Idiom

偃旗息鼓的意思是放倒军旗,停止击鼓,打造不准备战斗的假象;指不做声响,制造假象,迷惑对手。

This idiom originally referred to the act of lowering military banners and ceasing drumbeats to create an illusion of unpreparedness for battle. In a broader sense, it signifies the act of ceasing all activities and presenting an appearance of calmness and peace, with the intention of confusing or deceiving opponents.

4. 知识拓展 Knowledge Expansion

偃旗息鼓与空城计有异曲同工之妙。赵云和诸葛亮都是在敌强我弱的情况下,充分利用敌军统帅生性多疑的性格特点,避实就虚,通过虚张声势营造的氛围来干扰和影响对方,最终获得胜利。这个故事告诉我们:看事情不能只看表面,应该透过现象看本质;知己知彼,才能百战不殆。

The story of "lowering the banners and silencing the drums" bears a resemblance to the tale of the "empty city stratagem". Both narratives share a common principle. In the face of a stronger adversary, both Zhao Yun and Zhuge Liang astutely exploited the inherent suspicion of their enemy commanders. They skillfully created an illusionary atmosphere, using bravado and deception to disrupt and influence their opponents. Through this kind of cunning approach, they concealed their weaknesses, ultimately securing victory. This story serves as a reminder that appearances can be deceiving, and true insight lies in perceiving the essence beyond surface-level observations. Only by understanding ourselves and our adversaries can we navigate conflicts and emerge triumphant.

第六节
Section Six
———

鞠躬尽瘁，死而后已

Exerting One's Utmost Loyalty and Dedication, Even Beyond Death

1. 成语故事 The Story of the Idiom

三国时期，蜀主刘备死后，后主刘禅继位，把国内的军政大权交给诸葛亮。诸葛亮联吴伐魏，南征孟获，积极准备北伐。在最后一次北伐前夕，诸葛亮给刘禅上书《后出师表》，他对为什么必须北伐进行多重分析之后表示：所有的事都是很难预料的，战事更是最难以判断的，至于伐魏兴汉究竟是成功还是失败，是顺利还是困难，是自己所不能预见的；但是自己只有竭尽全力，到死方休，也就是要做到"鞠躬尽瘁，死而后已"。诸葛亮一生都在践行"鞠躬尽瘁，死而后已"，是中国忠臣与智者的代表人物。

During the Three Kingdoms Periods, after the death of Liu Bei, the founder of the Shu Kingdom, his son Liu Shan succeeded him and entrusted the military and political affairs to Zhuge Liang. Zhuge

045

Liang, in alliance with the Kingdom of Wu, waged wars against the Kingdom of Wei, conducted a successful southern expedition against Meng Huo, and prepared for the northern campaign. Prior to the final northern campaign, Zhuge Liang penned the "Second Memorial to the Throne" addressed to Liu Shan. In this memorial, he analyzed various factors and reasons for launching the northern campaign. Zhuge Liang expressed that many things are unpredictable, especially in warfare. Whether the expedition against the Kingdom of Wei and the restoration of the Han Dynasty would ultimately succeed or face difficulties remained uncertain. However, he stressed the importance of wholeheartedly dedicating himself to the cause, even to the point of death. The phrase "exerting one's utmost loyalty and dedication, even beyond death" perfectly captures Zhuge Liang's unwavering commitment to his duties. His loyalty and devotion epitomize the ideals of a loyal minister and wise strategist in China.

2.成语出处 The Source of the Idiom

诸葛亮在北伐之前给后主刘禅上书的表文《后出师表》："臣鞠躬尽瘁,死而后已;至于成败利钝,非臣之明所能逆睹也。"

This idiom originates from Zhuge Liang's "Second Memorial to the Throne", which he addressed to Liu Shan prior to his final northern expedition. In this memorial, Zhuge Liang expressed that the outcome of the expedition against the Kingdom of Wei and the restoration of the Han Dynasty was uncertain. However, he stressed the importance of wholeheartedly dedicating himself to the cause, even to the point of death.

3. 成语释义 Interpreting the Idiom

"鞠躬尽瘁，死而后已"的意思是勤勤恳恳，竭尽心力，到死为止；形容贡献全部的力量，至死方休。

This idiom signifies wholehearted dedication and giving one's utmost until death. It describes the act of contributing one's entire strength and persevering until the end.

4. 知识拓展 Knowledge Expansion

"鞠躬尽瘁，死而后已"所蕴含的精神已经成为中华民族宝贵的精神财富。在今日，我辈当以"鞠躬尽瘁，死而后已"的精神，勇于担当，奋发图强，为实现中华民族伟大复兴不断奋斗。

The spirit embodied in this idiom has become a kind of valuable spiritual treasure of the Chinese nation. In the present era, we should uphold this spirit, bravely shoulder responsibilities, and strive for excellence. Together, we can tirelessly work towards the rejuvenation of the Chinese nation.

第七节
Section Seven

七步成诗

Composing a Poem Within Seven Steps

1. 成语故事 The Story of the Idiom

曹丕在做了皇帝以后,对才华横溢的胞弟曹植一直心怀嫉恨。有一次,他命令曹植在大殿内走七步,然后以"兄弟"为题即兴吟诗一首,但诗中不能出现"兄弟"二字;写成则罢了,不成便要痛下杀手。曹植作出:"煮豆持作羹,漉菽以为汁。箕在釜下然,豆在釜中泣。本自同根生,相煎何太急?"这首脍炙人口的诗,因为是曹植在七步之内作成的,被后人称为《七步诗》。据说曹丕听了以后"深有惭色",不仅因为曹植在咏诗中展现的非凡才华令曹丕自愧不如,而且由于诗中浅显生动的比喻说明了兄弟本为手足、不应互相猜忌怨恨的大义。

After ascending the throne as emperor, Cao Pi harbored a deep resentment towards his talented younger brother, Cao Zhi. On one occasion, he commanded Cao Zhi to compose a poem on the spot with the theme of "brother" while taking seven steps in the grand hall. The condition was that the word "brother" should not appear in the poem, and failure to comply would result in dire consequences. Cao Zhi responded: "Cooking beans to make a broth, straining the bean juice. The husk burns beneath the cauldron, while tears fall from the beans within. From the same roots we sprout, why must we scorch each other?" This widely acclaimed poem, now known as the "Seven-Step Poem", earned its name for being composed within the span of seven steps. It is said that upon hearing it, Cao Pi was deeply moved and ashamed. Cao Zhi's exceptional talent shone through his verses, and the poignant metaphors conveyed the significance of brotherhood, urging Cao Pi to abandon suspicion and animosity.

2. 成语出处 The Source of the Idiom

南朝的刘义庆著的《世说新语·文学》："文帝尝令东阿王七步中作诗，不成者行大法。应声便为诗曰：'煮豆持作羹，漉菽以为汁。其在釜下然，豆在釜中泣。本自同根生，相煎何太急？'帝深有惭色。"

A New Account of the Tales of the World: Literary Talent written by Liu Yiqing during the Southern Dynasties: "Emperor Wen of Wei once ordered Lord Dong'e to compose a poem in seven steps, or face severe punishment. Lord Dong'e responded immediately with the following poem, 'Cooking beans to make a broth, straining the bean juice. The husk burns beneath the cauldron, while tears fall from the beans within. From the same roots we sprout, why must we scorch each other?' The emperor was so impressed by the poem that he was left in a state of profound shame."

3. 成语释义 Interpreting the Idiom

七步成诗比喻人的才思敏捷,知识渊博。

This idiom metaphorically describes someone who possesses agile thinking and extensive knowledge.

4. 知识拓展 Knowledge Expansion

曹植作的《七步诗》共六句,后人缩减为四句,流传更广。

The "Seven-Step Poem" written by Cao Zhi originally consisted of six lines, but it was later condensed to four lines by later generations. The shortened version became more widely circulated.

《七步诗》(由后人缩写)

煮豆燃豆萁,豆在釜中泣。

本自同根生,相煎何太急?

Seven-Step Poem(The shortened version)

Cook beans, burn bean husks,

Beans weep inside the cauldron.

Born from the same roots,

Why rush to scorch each other?

Section Eight

乐不思蜀

Indulge in Pleasures and Forget Home

1. 成语故事 The Story of the Idiom

　　蜀汉后主刘禅是一位非常无能的君主,加上连年征战,蜀国的国力逐渐衰弱。魏国大将钟会、邓艾率两路大军进攻蜀国,一路势如破竹。姜维在剑阁与钟会对垒,而邓艾险出奇兵暗度阴平,破江油得绵竹,逼入锦官城。刘禅无奈反绑双臂,叫人捧着玉玺,出宫投降。蜀国灭亡之后,司马昭把刘禅安排到魏国的都城居住,同时为了笼络人心,还封他为安乐公。司马昭虽然知道刘禅无能,但还是要探一探他的虚实。有一次,司马昭设宴款待刘禅,先是安排魏国歌舞表演,随同投降的原蜀国臣子看后都非常感伤,而刘禅看后却面露喜色。然后他又安排人表演蜀国的乐曲歌舞,原蜀臣们不由得想起国破家亡,个个泪流满面,而唯独刘禅依旧嬉笑自若。司马昭见状便问刘禅:"你是否很思念蜀国呢?"贪图安乐的刘禅答道:"这个地方令人快乐,我并不思念蜀国。"这就是"乐不思蜀"典故的由来。

Liu Shan, the later ruler of Shu, was a highly incompetent monarch. After years of war, the strength of Shu gradually declined, providing an opportunity for the formidable Wei generals, Zhong Hui and Deng Ai, to invade Shu with ease. Zhong Hui confronted Jiang Wei at Jian'ge, while Deng Ai employed unexpected tactics to cross the Yinping Mountains, capturing Jiangyou and Mianzhu, and advancing towards Jin'guan City, the capital of Shu. Faced with no other options, Liu Shan reluctantly bound himself and surrendered, symbolizing his submission with the presentation of the imperial seal. After the downfall of Shu, Sima Zhao relocated Liu Shan to the Wei capital and, in an attempt to win favor, conferred upon him the title of Duke of An'le. Although Sima Zhao was aware of Liu Shan's incompetence, he sought to test Liu Shan's true feelings. At a banquet, Sima Zhao first arranged the performance of Wei's songs and dances, which deeply saddened the former Shu ministers who had surrendered. However, Liu Shan displayed delight. Following this, Shu's music and dances were performed, evoking tears and nostalgia among the former Shu ministers, who reminisced about their fallen homeland. Yet Liu Shan remained lighthearted and unaffected. Witnessing this, Sima Zhao inquired, "Do you miss Shu?" To which the pleasure-seeking Liu Shan replied, "This place is so joyful that I do not miss Shu at all." Thus, the idiom "indulge in pleasures and forget home" originated.

2. 成语出处 The Source of the Idiom

《三国志 · 蜀书 · 后主传》,裴松之注引《汉晋春秋》:"问禅曰:'颇思蜀否?'禅曰:'此间乐,不思蜀。'"

The Records of the Three Kingdoms — The Book of Shu: A Biography of the Later Ruler, Pei Songzhi cited the *Book of Later Han and Jin Dynasty* when he wrote: "Sima Zhao asked Liu Shan, 'Do you miss Shu?' Liu Shan replied, 'This place is so joyful that I do not miss Shu at all.'"

3. 成语释义 Interpreting the Idiom

乐不思蜀的字面意思是很快乐，不思念蜀国；比喻在新环境中获得乐趣，不想回到原来的环境；也比喻沉迷于现有状况，忘记曾经的志向，不思进取。与其意思相近的成语有流连忘返。

The literal meaning of this idiom is "being joyful and not missing Shu". It metaphorically signifies finding happiness in a new environment and no longer yearning for the past. It also implies becoming engrossed in the current situation, forgetting one's original ambitions, and lacking the motivation to progress. A similar idiom is "being captivated and forgetting to return".

4. 知识拓展 Knowledge Expansion

都城汴梁被金人攻陷后，宋徽宗、宋钦宗被俘虏，中原被金人侵占。赵构逃到江南，在临安即位，建立南宋。南宋朝廷并没有吸取北宋亡国的惨痛教训而发愤图强，不思收复中原失地，但求苟且偏安。达官显贵一味纵情声色，寻欢作乐。南宋诗人林升创作一首七绝《题临安邸》："山外青山楼外楼，西湖歌舞几时休？暖风熏得游人醉，直把杭州作汴州。"这首诗就是对当时政治环境和社会现状的讽刺，表达了诗人的愤激之情。

After the capital of Bianliang was captured by the Jin people, the emperors of the Northern Song Dynasty, Song Huizong and Song Qinzong, were taken as captives, and the territory of the Central Plains fell under Jin's rule. Zhao Gou, known as Song Gaozong, fled to the south and established his reign in Lin'an, marking the beginning of the Southern Song Dynasty. However, the members of the ruling class of the Southern Song failed to learn from the tragic lessons of the downfall of the Northern Song. Instead of striving to reclaim the lost lands of the Central Plains, they sought temporary peace and security. The ruling elites indulged in hedonistic pleasures and revelries. In response to this political and social environment, the Southern Song poet Lin Sheng composed a seven-character quatrain, titled "Inscription at an Inn of Lin'an". The poem read: "Beyond green mountains, towers rise upon towers; When will the revelry by West Lake's shore finally cease? The warm breeze lures wanderers into a drunken state; Mistaking Hangzhou for Bianzhou that's been seized." This poem serves as a satire, expressing the poet's frustration and indignation towards the prevailing circumstances.

汉中成语典故悦读

Enchanting Tales of Idioms from Hanzhong

第一节

Section One

千金一笑

The Beacon Fires that Laughter Lit

1. 成语故事 The Story of the Idiom

西周君主周幽王在位时，地震、干旱等自然灾害频发。周幽王不但不体恤民情，反而变本加厉地剥削百姓，还重用奸佞之徒，引起国人怨愤。褒姒是古褒国一名女子，周幽王见其容貌出众，乃纳她为妃，后立为后。（古褒国遗址位于今天汉中市河东店镇的周寨附近。如今那里还有一个叫褒姒铺的地方，被称为褒姒故里。）周幽王非常宠爱褒姒，但褒姒总是皱着眉头。周幽王想尽办法引她发笑，她却没有笑过一回。于是周幽王派人贴出告示：谁能让褒姒一笑，就可以得到千两金子。许多人都来尝试，可没有一个人成功。有一天，一名大臣虢石父想出了一个主意，周幽王表示要试一试。为博褒姒一笑，周幽王带褒姒来到骊山，命人燃起了烽火。附近的诸侯看到了警报，以为敌兵来了，就急忙带兵赶去援助。可到了骊山下，一个敌人都没看到，却听到了山上的鼓乐之声，大家都愣住了。周幽王便派人告诉他们："不过是大王和王妃点烽火玩，你们回去吧。"诸侯这才知道上了大王的当，十分愤怒，就各自带兵回去了。褒姒见到这场面却笑了起来。周幽王很高兴，因而又命人多次点燃烽火。后来，周幽王废黜了王后申后及太子，申后的父亲申侯联合缯国和西夷犬戎攻打周国。周幽王得知他们攻打都城镐京，惊慌失措，急忙下令把骊山的烽火点燃，以求诸侯前来救援。尽管烽火台上连燃烽火告急，诸侯都认为这仍是周幽王在作乐，就没理会。结果，犬戎军队攻入镐京，杀死了周幽王，西周灭亡。这就是中国历史上"烽火戏诸侯"的故事。

During the reign of Emperor Zhou You of the Western Zhou Dynasty, the land was plagued by natural disasters such as earthquakes and droughts. Rather than comforting his people, Emperor Zhou You exacerbated their sufferings by intensifying exploitation and favoring treacherous ministers. This caused widespread resentments among the populace. Bao Si, a woman from the ancient state of Bao, caught the king's eye with her exceptional beauty and finally became his queen. (The ruins of the ancient state of Bao is located near the present-day Hedongdian Town in Hanzhong City, and there remains a place called Bao Si's posthouse, which is known as her hometown.) Despite Emperor Zhou You's deep affection for Bao Si, she always wore a frown. The king tried various ways to make her smile, but his attempts were in vain. In a bid, Emperor Zhou You issued a proclamation offering a reward of a thousand pieces of gold to anyone who could make her smile. Many people tried, but none succeeded. One day, a minister named Guo Shifu came up with an idea, and Emperor Zhou You decided to give it a try. To provoke Bao Si's laughter, Emperor Zhou You took her to Mount Li and ordered to set the beacon fires. When neighboring vassals saw the signal, they thought it was a sign of enemy invasion and rushed to Mount Li to provide assistance. However, upon reaching the foot of Mount Li, they found no enemy, only the sound of drums and music coming from the mountaintop. They were bewildered. Emperor Zhou You sent someone to inform them, "It's just the king and queen enjoying the beacon fires. You may return." The vassals realized they had been deceived and were filled with anger, so they returned to their own territories. Bao Si, witnessing this scene, finally laughed. Emperor Zhou You was delighted and ordered to light the beacon fires multiple times to see her laughter. Later, Emperor Zhou You deposed Queen Shen and the crown prince. In response, Marquis Shen, the father of Queen Shen, joined forces with the Zeng State and the western tribes of Quanrong people to attack the Western Zhou. Upon hearing the news of the impending attack on the capital city of Haojing, Emperor Zhou You panicked and urgently ordered the beacon fires to be lit, hoping to summon assistance from the vassals. However, the vassals, believing it to be another trick, did not come to his aid this time. As a result, the Quanrong army breached Haojing, killed Emperor Zhou You. The Western Zhou Dynasty collapsed. This is the story of "tricking the vassals with beacon fires" in Chinese history.

2. 成语出处 The Source of the Idiom

《史记·周本纪》:"褒姒不好笑,幽王欲其笑万方,故不笑。幽王为烽燧大鼓,有寇至则举烽火。诸侯悉至,至而无寇,褒姒乃大笑。幽王说之,为数举烽火。其后不信,诸侯益亦不至……申侯怒,与缯、西夷犬戎攻幽王。幽王举烽火征兵,兵莫至。遂杀幽王骊山下,掳褒姒,尽取周赂而去。"

Records of the Grand Historian: The Zhou Dynasty: "Bao Si always wore a frown, and Emperor Zhou You was determined to make her smile, but she refused. In order to achieve his goal, Emperor Zhou You decided to use lighting beacon fires and beating drums as the signal to alert the vassals of a potential enemy invasion. When the vassals saw the beacon signal, they promptly went to provide assistance. However, when they arrived, they found no enemy; instead, they witnessed Bao Si laughing heartily. Emperor Zhou You was delighted by her laughter and continued to light the beacon fires, hoping to see her laughter again. However, as time passed, the vassals began to doubt the credibility of this signal and stopped coming to his aid ... In a fit of anger, Marquis Shen allied with the Zeng State and the western tribes of Quanrong people to attack the Western Zhou. Desperate for help, Emperor Zhou You ordered the beacon fires to be lit, calling for reinforcements, but not a single soldier came to his rescue. In the end, Emperor Zhou You was killed at the foot of Mount Li; Bao Si was captured; and the properties were taken."

3. 成语释义 Interpreting the Idiom

千金一笑，也作千金买笑，指不惜重金博取美人欢心，也指美人笑之难得。

This idiom, also known as "spending a fortune to buy a smile", refers to the act of going to great lengths to win the favor of a beautiful woman. It implies that a beautiful woman's smile is rare and precious.

4. 知识拓展 Knowledge Expansion

（1）随着历史学家详细深入的研究，现在已经有学者质疑，认为"烽火戏诸侯"没有历史依据,更像是古人编造的故事。然而无论故事是真或是假,"烽火戏诸侯"只不过是西周灭亡的一个象征,真正导致西周灭亡的原因是统治者的残暴、荒淫无度和失信于民。

After extensive and in-depth researches by historians, some scholars have raised doubts about the historical authenticity of the tale "tricking the vassals with beacon fires". They argue that the story lacks sufficient evidence and may have been a fabrication from ancient times. However, regardless of its historical veracity, the story served as a symbolic representation of the decline of the Western Zhou Dynasty. The true factors that led to the downfall of the Western Zhou Dynasty were the rulers' cruelty, extravagance, and betrayal of the people's trust.

(2)像古希腊作品《伊索寓言》中记载的《狼来了》的故事一样,谎话说多了自然无人再信,最后会失去周围人的信任并自食恶果。

Similar to the story "The Boy Who Cried Wolf" in the ancient Greek work *Aesop's Fables*, when a person tells lies repeatedly, people will no longer trust him. This can have severe repercussions as he risks losing the trust and support of those around.

第二节
Section Two

一人得道，鸡犬升天

When a Man Succeeds, All His Friends and Relatives Get Favor

1. 成语故事 The Story of the Idiom

西汉末年，一个名叫唐公房的人在汉中郡衙（今汉中市城固县许家庙）做官，他既爱学道，又酷爱种植柑橘。他所务橘园，绕河之水，沐山神风，所产蜜橘甘甜味美。一天，唐公房偶然遇到一位修仙得道的真人，便拜这位真人为师，此后便潜心钻研道学，并经常给师傅送去鲜美的柑橘品尝。真人感受到了唐公房的诚心，就赐给他仙丹。唐公房服了仙丹之后，瞬间拥有了诸多本领，如能辨别鸟兽的语言，还能行走如飞，数百里外的郡府转眼就能抵达。乡亲们和郡守都十分惊讶。汉中郡守遂跟着唐公房学道，但始终不得其法，就以为是唐公房故意留有一手而不教，恼怒之下派兵去捉拿唐公房及其家人。一位好心人意外听到了这一消息，赶在兵到之前告诉了唐公房这一祸事。唐公房得知这一情况就告诉师父。真人说：“吾徒不必惊慌，为师送你仙丹。你们食用后，便可飞天而去，逃离厄运。”唐公房及其家人服用了真人给的仙丹后就飞天而去。由于唐妻留恋其房舍及禽畜，真人又给房屋施了仙术。同时家里的鸡、狗、猪等喝了主人喝仙丹剩下的水也都一起飞上了天。顷刻间，房屋、牲畜倏然而去，连同唐公房的果园都飞升上天。于是有了"鸡鸣天空""狗吠云中"的奇景。后来，当地百姓建造"灵寿宫"为之祭祀，后将其改名为"唐仙观"；同时，所在的村子也被称为"升仙村"。

During the late Western Han Dynasty, a man named Tang Gongfang held an official position in Hanzhong (now in Xujia Temple, Chenggu County, Hanzhong City), and was passionate about Taoism studies and orange cultivation. His orange grove, surrounded by flowing water and embraced by mountain breezes, yielded delicious and sweet fruits. One day, Tang Gongfang met a true Taoist immortal. He was so impressed by the immortal's wisdom that he decided to become his disciple. Tang immersed himself in the study of Taoism and often presented his master with exquisite oranges to enjoy. Recognizing Tang Gongfang's sincerity, the Taoist immortal gifted him with an elixir. After taking the elixir, Tang gained extraordinary abilities. He could understand the language of animals and traverse great distances with incredible speed. News of his remarkable talents spread, astounding both his fellow villagers and the local county magistrate. The magistrate was eager to learn from Tang, but he struggled to grasp the teachings imparted by his mentor. Suspecting that Tang intentionally withheld certain knowledge, the magistrate grew angry and ordered his soldiers to apprehend Tang and his family. Fortunately, a kind-hearted man overheard the news and alerted Tang in advance. Tang sought guidance from his master, who assured him, saying, "Do not panic. I shall give you and your family another elixir. Once consumed, you will be able to ascend up to the sky and escape your misfortune." Tang and his family consumed the elixir and flied up to heaven. Since Tang's wife was worried about their home and livestock, the immortal gave a magical enchantment. Their chickens, dogs, and pigs lapped up the remaining elixir-infused water and joined them in the sky. In an instant, their house, animals, and even Tang's orchard ascended up to the heaven, creating a wondrous sight of chickens crowing in the sky and dogs barking among the clouds. The local residents built a temple in honor of Tang Gongfang. Originally called Lingshou Palace, the temple came to be known as the Tang Immortal Temple. The village itself was also renamed "Becoming Immortal Village".

2.成语出处 The Source of the Idiom

北魏地理学家郦道元的地理巨著《水经注》和宋代文学家欧阳修的《欧阳文忠集》中,也都对这个成语典故有所记载。原存于城固县的《仙人唐公房碑》专门记述了这个故事,该碑现保存在西安碑林博物馆。

This idiom originates from a story recorded in two renowned works: the geographical masterpiece *Shui Jing Zhu* by the geographer Li Daoyuan from the Northern Wei Dynasty, and the literary collection *Ouyang Wenzhong Ji* by the Song Dynasty writer Ouyang Xiu. The tale is also inscribed on the Immortal Tang Gongfang's Stele, initially situated in Chenggu County and presently kept in the Xi'an Beilin Museum.

3.成语释义 Interpreting the Idiom

"一人得道，鸡犬升天"，也作"一人得道，仙及鸡犬"，意思是一个人得道成仙，全家连鸡、狗也都随之升天；比喻一个人做了官，和他有关系的人也都跟着得势。

This idiom conveys the meaning that when a person achieves enlightenment and becomes immortal, his entire family, including even the chickens and dogs, ascend up to the heaven. It is a metaphor for a situation where a person attains an official position, and those associated with him also benefit and rise in influence.

4.现实意义 Practical Significant

"一人得道，鸡犬升天"在古代是一种常见的社会现象。一个人凭自身的才能得到朝廷的赏识，就改变了命运，与他有关系的人也都跟着沾光。但俗话说得好——"祸兮福所倚，福兮祸所伏"，与其相对的就是"一人落败，满门抄斩"。真是一荣俱荣，一损俱损。

The social phenomenon reflected by this idiom was prevalent in ancient China. If a person's talents were recognized and appreciated by the court, it would alter his destiny. Those closely associated with him would also benefit from his success. However, there is a saying goes, "Misfortune may be a disguise for fortune, and fortune may be a disguise for misfortune." This is also exemplified by a corresponding idom, that the downfall of one person would result in the decimation of his entire family. They serve as powerful reminders that fortunes and misfortunes are shared collectively.

第三节

Section Three

廉泉让水

Lianquan River and Rang River

1.成语故事 The Story of the Idiom

南北朝时,梁州辖今陕南、四川、黔北等广大地区,梁州城设在南郑(今汉中市汉台区)。一次,梁州州将刘亮派范柏年进京觐见宋明帝。明帝与范柏年闲谈时,问他:"爱卿,广州有水,名曰贪泉。据说那里出的贪官均与饮此水有关。此事你可听说过?"不等范柏年回答,明帝又一语双关地问道:"梁州是否有这种地名?"范柏年稍加考虑后答道:"圣上明察,梁州唯有文川、武乡、廉泉、让水。"(廉泉、让水为古水名。"廉泉"现称濂水河,位于今陕西省汉中市南郑区濂水镇;"让水"位于今陕西省汉中市汉台区武乡镇。)明帝再问:"爱卿宅居何处?"范伯年答:"微臣寒舍居于廉、让之间。"范柏年巧妙对答,无懈可击,既说明他任职之地民风淳朴、百姓谦逊,又暗示自己为政清廉。这就是"廉泉让水"典故的由来。此后,"廉泉让水"成为民风淳朴、为官清廉的代名词。

During the Southern and Northern Dynasties, Liangzhou governed a vast area including present-day southern Shaanxi, Sichuan, and northern Guizhou. The capital of Liangzhou was located in Nanzheng (now a part of the Hantai District in Hanzhong City). On one occasion, the Liangzhou general Liu Liang sent Fan Bainian to the capital to present himself before the Emperor Ming of Song. During their conversation, the emperor asked Fan, "My minister, is there a water source named Tan Spring in Guangzhou? It is said that corrupt officials in that area are related to drinking from this spring. Have you heard of such a thing?" Before Fan could respond, the emperor posed another question involving a pun, asking, "Does Liangzhou have a place with a similar name?" After careful consideration, Fan replied, "Your Majesty, with your keen insight, Liangzhou has only Wenchuan, Wuxiang, Lianquan River, and Rang River." (Lianquan River and Rang River were names of ancient water. Lianquan River is now known as the Lianshui River, located in Lianshui Town, Nanzheng District, Hanzhong City, Shaanxi Province. Rang River is currently located in Wuxiang Town, Hantai District, Hanzhong City, Shaanxi Province.) The emperor then asked Fan about his place of residence. Fan replied, "Your humble servant resides between Lianquan River and Rang River." Fan's skillful response not only indicated the simplicity and humility of the people in his assigned region, but also implied his own dedication to clean and upright governance. This is the origin of the idiom "Lianquan River and Rang River". Later, it represents the virtues of simplicity and integrity in both civilians and government officials.

067

2.成语出处 The Source of the Idiom

《南史·胡谐之传》："帝言次及广州贪泉，因问柏年：'卿州复有此水不？'答曰：'梁州唯有文川、武乡、廉泉、让水。'"

The History of the Southern Dynasties: A Biography of Hu Xiezhi: "During the emperor's discussion about the existence of Tan Spring in Guangzhou, he enquired of Bainian, 'My minister, does Liangzhou also have a water source called Tan Spring?' To this, Fan Bainian responded, 'Liangzhou has only Wenchuan, Wuxiang, Lianquan River, and Rang River.'"

3.成语释义 Interpreting the Idiom

"廉泉""让水"本是两条河流的名称，人们赋予它们以"廉洁"和"谦让"的美好品格。"廉泉让水"原比喻为官廉洁，后来也比喻风土习俗淳美。其近义词有两袖清风、一琴一鹤、一廉如水。

"Lianquan River" and "Rang River" were originally the names of two rivers. However, people have endowed them with the noble qualities of "integrity" and "modesty". This idiom originally referred to the integrity of officials. It later came to represent the purity of local customs and traditions. Some synonyms for this idiom are as follows: "having clean sleeves" (a Chinese idiom that means to be incorruptible and honest), "a *qin* and a crane" (a Chinese idiom that means to be a scholar who lives a simple and elegant life; the *qin* is a Chinese stringed instrument, and the crane is a symbol of longevity and wisdom; this idiom is often used to describe people who are wise, cultured, and incorruptible), "as pure as water" (a common idiom that means to be honest and without corruption, is derived from the fact that water is clear and pure, and is often used to describe people who are honest and upright).

4.知识拓展 Knowledge Expansion

（1）据《晋书·吴隐之传》记载，广州城外二十里，有一眼著名的泉水，名曰贪泉，意思是人饮其水即起贪心，即使廉士亦贪。因此，过路之人即使口干舌燥，望泉而过，也不敢擅自饮用。但是东晋新上任的广州刺史吴隐之，到广州首先喝了贪泉之水，并说："为官贪廉与泉水何干？"他还作诗言志："古人云此水，一歃重千金。若使夷齐饮，终当不易心。"（其意思是人们说饮了贪泉之水就会变成贪官，但如果让伯夷、叔齐这样的清廉者饮用，他们是绝对不会变得贪恋钱财的。）吴隐之担任广州刺史期间，始终保持不贪不占的清白操行。任期满后，他从广州乘船返回建康时，依然身无长物，两袖清风。

According to the biography of Wu Yinzhi in the *Book of Jin*, there was a famous spring called Tan Spring located 10 kilometers outside the city of Guangzhou. Its name implied that drinking its water would induce greed, even among virtuous individuals. Passersby refrained from drinking from the spring, even if they were thirsty. However, when Wu Yinzhi arrived in Guangzhou as the newly appointed governor during the Eastern Jin Dynasty, he made a bold move. He drank from Tan Spring and defiantly declared, "What does being an official have to do with the water's tendency to arouse greed?" He even composed a poem to express his aspirations, stating, "People claim that drinking from Tan Spring turns one into a corrupt official, but if virtuous individuals like Boyi and Shuqi were to drink from it, they would never become obsessed with wealth." Wu Yinzhi maintained the principled and upright conduct during his tenure as the governor of Guangzhou, free from greed or exploitation. When his term came to an end, he returned to Jiankang from Guangzhou by boat, with nothing to his name and remaining uncorrupted.

（2）清代诗人黄作柽曾作有《廉泉让水歌》一首，其后几句为："世风习贪诈，溪壑嗟难填。渴害心为害，尘襟谁涤涧？我愿来此地，卜居远市廛。置身廉让间，仰企范柏年。"这首诗表达了诗人对世风日下、贪诈横溢、私欲难涤的社会现状的愤叹，表明自己愿意效法范氏超脱污浊、保持清廉的态度。

During the Qing Dynasty, the poet Huang Zuocheng composed a poem titled "Song of Lianquan River and Rang River". The concluding lines of the poem are as follows: "In this corrupt world, deceit and greed prevail, leaving the valleys and streams lamenting. When avarice corrupts the heart, who can cleanse their worldly desires? I aspire to come to this place, to live far from bustling markets. Embracing the virtues of honesty and humility, I look up to the example set by Fan Bainian." This poem expresses the poet's lamentation about the deteriorating moral values and rampant greed in society, where personal desires are hard to purify. It unveils the poet's resolve to follow in the footsteps of Fan Bainian, transcending impurities and embracing a life of integrity.

（3）在吟咏"廉泉让水"的同时，也出现了一个有趣的现象。人们开始反思传说中泉水的功能和品性，为"贪泉"正名。人的廉贪不是由饮廉、贪二水而决定，完全是由自己的行为决定的，泉水不应为人的行为担责。如宋人阮阅的七言绝句《郴江百咏》就表达了这一观点：

玉洁冰寒彻底清，不因汲引有亏盈。

廉泉让水贪无异，空使时人恶此名。

With numerous poems that describe the "Lianquan River and Rang River", an interesting phenomenon arises. People begin to reflect on the function and nature of the legendary spring, seeking to vindicate "Tan Spring". They realize that one's integrity is not determined by drinking from "Tan" or "Lian" waters; it is solely determined by one's own actions. The spring/water should not be tarnished or praised by the reputation of human behavior. For instance, in the seven-character quatrain "One Hundred Songs of Chen River" by the Song Dynasty poet Ruan Yue, this idea is depicted:

Jade-like clarity, ice-cold chill,

A spring that never runs dry or overflows.

Lianquan River and Rang River are both pure,

It's the people of the time who malign the name.

（4）汉中博物馆西大门外就曾贴有关于廉泉让水的楹联："文川武乡英雄地,让水廉泉礼仪邦"。在此地悬贴这副楹联,赞美汉中人才济济、民风淳朴,可谓意义深远。

Outside the west gate of the Hanzhong Museum, there used to be a couplet related to this idiom: "Wenchuan and Wuxiang, the land of heroes; Rang River and Lianquan River, the realm of etiquette". This couplet at this place praises the abundance of talent and the simplicity of the people in Hanzhong, making it of profound significance.

第四节
Section Four

胸有成竹

Bamboos in Mind Before Painting

1. 成语故事 The Story of the Idiom

文同，北宋著名画家、诗人，尤其擅长画竹，曾先后任兴元府（今汉中市）知府、洋州（今汉中市洋县）知州。文同清廉爱民、兴利除弊、才学卓越，在当地深得人心。文同在汉中为官五年，留下诗作几百首，其中兴元诗 93 首、洋州诗 162 首，他对汉中的热爱之情可见一斑。文同毕生喜竹、尊竹、赞竹、画竹，自称"嗜竹种复画"，在当时享有盛名。洋州城北有筼筜谷（今洋县纸坊乡砚台山与文家坪之间），茂林修竹，文同闲暇之余常去那里观竹、画竹。经过多年的观竹与画竹，文同终于悟出了画竹的真谛。文同画竹的原理与技法后来衍化成脍炙人口的成语"胸有成竹"，因此也有"胸有成竹"源自汉中的说法。

Wen Tong, also known as Wen Yuke, was a renowned painter

and poet of the Northern Song Dynasty. He was particularly skilled in painting bamboos. Throughout his career, he held the positions of Governor of Xingyuan Prefecture (now Hanzhong City) and Governor of Yangzhou (now Yangxian County, Hanzhong City). Wen Tong was known for his integrity, compassion for the people, dedication to reforms, and exceptional talent, which earning him great popularity in local area. During his five-year tenure in Hanzhong, Wen Tong left behind a collection of hundreds of poems, with 93 dedicated to Xingyuan and 162 to Yangzhou. These poems demonstrated his deep affection for Hanzhong. Wen Tong was a lifelong enthusiast of bamboos, both in his admiration for bamboos and his artistic portrayal of bamboos. He often referred to himself as someone who loved, cultivated, and painted bamboos repeatedly. This passion earned him widespread acclaim. Wen Tong would frequently visit Yundang Valley (now located between Yantai Mountain and Wenjiaping in Zhifang Township, Yangxian County), a place with lush forests and tall bamboos, to observe and paint bamboos. Years of immersing himself in the study and depiction of bamboos allowed Wen Tong to grasp the essence of painting bamboos. One of the most famous idioms associated with Wen Tong is "bamboos in mind before painting". This idiom emphasizes the importance of thorough preparation and a clear vision when creating art. Hence, there is a saying that this idiom originated from Hanzhong.

2.成语出处 The Source of the Idiom

故事出自北宋苏轼的散文《文与可画筼筜谷偃竹记》。文同与苏轼是忘年之交,两人惺惺相惜,情谊深厚。苏轼在《文与可画筼筜谷偃竹记》中这样描写文同画竹:"故画竹必先得成竹于胸中,执笔熟视,乃见其所欲画者,急起从之,振笔直遂,以追其所见,如兔起鹘落,少纵则逝矣。"

The story originates from Su Shi's prose "Recording How Wen Yuke Paints Bamboos in Yundang Valley", which was written during the Northern Song Dynasty. Despite the age difference, Wen Tong and Su Shi shared close and deeply cherished friendship. In his prose, Su Shi vividly portrayed Wen Tong's approach to painting bamboos: "When painting bamboos, Wen Tong first visualizes the complete image of the bamboos in his mind. He will hold the brush carefully and observe the bamboos before making a single stroke. Swiftly and confidently, he follows the mental image, capturing it with a single stroke of the brush, akin to a rabbit leaping or a falcon diving, fleeting if hesitated even slightly."

3. 成语释义 Interpreting the Idiom

胸有成竹原指画竹子前要在心里先有竹子的形象,后来比喻在做事之前已经拿定主意。

The idiom originally refers to the need to have a mental image of the bamboos in order to paint bamboos accurately. It later comes to mean making a firm decision before undertaking a task.

4. 知识拓展 Knowledge Expansion

胸有成竹也写作成竹在胸,其同义词有胜券在握、心中有数,其反义词有惊慌失措、茫无头绪、心中无数。

Synonyms of this idiom include "victory is assured" and "have a clear understanding in mind". Its antonyms include "in a state of panic", "at a loss", and "having no clue".

两汉三国历史故事戏剧悦读

Theatrical Delights: Historical Stories from the Western Han, Eastern Han, and Three Kingdoms

第一节
Section One

———

鸿门宴

The Hongmen Feast

一、故事梗概 Synopsis

秦末,刘邦与项羽各自率军反秦。刘邦的兵力虽不及项羽的,但刘邦先破咸阳,驻军霸上,并派兵驻守函谷关。项羽闻后攻克函谷关,进入咸阳,大军驻扎在新丰鸿门。刘邦的左司马曹无伤向项羽告密,说刘邦打算在关中称王。项羽听后勃然大怒,准备讨伐刘邦。听到这个消息后,刘邦自认不是项羽的对手,就到鸿门向项羽告罪并解释缘由。鸿门宴上,虽有美酒佳肴,但杀机重重,影响历史走向的一场大幕就此拉开。

The Qin Dynasty ended with Liu Bang and Xiang Yu leading their respective armies in the attacks against the Qin Empire. Liu Bang's army was smaller, but it managed to breach the defenses in the city of Xianyang and establish a base in Bashang. Liu Bang also stationed troops to guard the Hangu Pass. Upon learning of this, Xiang Yu successfully captured the Hangu Pass and entered Xianyang. He established his army's presence in Hongmen, Xinfeng. It was during this time that Liu Bang's subordinate, the Left Defender-in-Chief Cao Wushang, betrayed him. He informed Xiang Yu of Liu Bang's intention to become the King of Guanzhong. Enraged by this news, Xiang Yu swiftly mobilized his forces to suppress Liu Bang. Realizing that he himself was no match for Xiang Yu, Liu Bang went to Hongmen, apologized to Xiang Yu and confessed his guilt. The Hongmen feast took place, with lavish wine and exquisite food, yet an undercurrent of impending danger loomed. It was a pivotal moment in Chinese history.

二、戏剧舞台 Theatre Stages

第一幕

Act 1

———

项羽欲攻刘邦　项伯告密张良

Xiang Yu Intends to Attack Liu Bang;
Xiang Bo Informs Zhang Liang

【人物】　项羽、刘邦、张良、范增、项伯、曹无伤、侍卫

【Characters】　Xiang Yu, Liu Bang, Zhang Liang, Fan Zeng, Xiang Bo, Cao Wushang, Guards

【场景】　项羽营帐

【Scene】　Xiang Yu's camp

【剧本】

【Script】

旁白：秦朝末年，刘邦、项羽起兵反秦。刘邦的兵力少于项羽的，刘邦却率先攻入咸阳。刘邦的左司马曹无伤来到项羽营寨向项羽告密。

Narrator: During the later years of the Qin Dynasty, Liu Bang and Xiang Yu rise up in rebellion against the Qin regime. Despite having a smaller army, Liu Bang manages to seize the city of Xianyang before Xiang Yu. Now, Cao Wushang, the Left Defender-in-Chief under Liu Bang, arrives at Xiang Yu's camp and betrays Liu Bang by revealing crucial information.

侍卫：报！曹无伤求见！

Guards: General! Cao Wushang is outside requesting to report to you!

项羽：传！

Xiang Yu: Bring him in!

曹无伤：启禀项王，沛公先您攻入咸阳，想要在关中称王，让子婴做丞相，珍宝全都被他占有了。

Cao Wushang: My Lord, I bring news. Liu Bang has gone ahead and breached the defense of Xianyang. He intends to proclaim himself king in Guanzhong and appoint Ziying as prime minister. He has also claimed the city's treasures for himself.

项羽：（大怒）刘邦竟如此胆大！

Xiang Yu: (Enraged) How dare Liu Bang!

范增：沛公目前势力不大，但欲望不小，现在赶快攻打，不要错失良机。

Fan Zeng: Liu Bang has his limitations, but we can't ignore his desire for power. We must strike now and not let this opportunity slip away.

项羽：好，明天犒劳士兵，准备攻打刘邦。

Xiang Yu: Very well. Tomorrow we shall reward our soldiers and then prepare for an attack on Liu Bang.

旁白：项羽的叔父项伯与刘邦的谋士张良是故交，张良曾救过项伯。项伯知道项羽要攻打刘邦后，连夜骑马赶到刘邦军营，秘密会见张良，劝其离开。张良认为现在沛公遇到危急的事，逃走是不守信义的。

Narrator: Xiang Bo, Xiang Yu's uncle, is a close friend of Zhang Liang, one of Liu Bang's strategists who had once saved Xiang Bo. After learning of Liu Bang's predicament, Xiang Bo rides through the night to Liu Bang's camp, and secretly meets with Zhang Liang and urges him to leave. However, Zhang Liang believes that abandoning his lord in such a critical time would be an act of betrayal.

刘邦：(听到报告后惊慌不已)这该怎么办呢？

Liu Bang: (In a panicked state after receiving the report) What should I do?

张良：我为您引见项伯，我们一起商量一下。

Zhang Liang: Let me introduce Xiang Bo to you; together we can discuss our course of action.

刘邦：他在哪里？

Liu Bang: Where is he?

张良：他此刻正在帐外。

Zhang Liang: He is waiting outside the camp.

刘邦：请他进来。

Liu Bang: Please bring him in.

项伯：见过沛公。

Xiang Bo: Greetings, Duke of Pei.

刘邦：谢谢你告知我此事。我觉得我和项王之间有些误会。

Liu Bang: Thank you for informing me of this. I think there has been a misunderstanding between King Xiang and I.

项伯：什么误会？

Xiang Bo: A misunderstanding?

刘邦：我虽先入咸阳，但分毫未取。我令士兵驻守咸阳只是为了防止意外发生。我日夜渴望项王来咸阳，怎么会背叛他呢？

Liu Bang: Yes. I entered Xianyang first, but I did not take a single thing for myself. I ordered my soldiers to guard the city simply to prevent any mishaps. I have been eagerly awaiting King Xiang's arrival in Xianyang. How could I possibly betray him?

项伯：现在我了解情况了，我将如实向项王禀告。不过你必须尽早向项王说明一切。

Xiang Bo: I understand. I will pass this message to King Xiang. However, you must explain everything to him yourself as soon as possible.

刘邦：好，那就按你所说的做。

Liu Bang: Understood. I will heed your counsel and provide him with a thorough explanation without delay.

第二幕

Act 2

———

项庄舞剑，意在沛公

Xiang Zhuang's Sword Dance: A Deceptive Cover

for His Assassination Attempt on Liu Bang's Life

【人物】 项羽、项伯、刘邦、范增、项庄、张良

【Characters】 Xiang Yu, Xiang Bo, Liu Bang, Fan Zeng, Xiang Zhuang, Zhang Liang

【场景】 鸿门宴会

【Scene】 Hongmen banquet

【剧本】

【Script】

旁白：项王设宴。项羽、项伯朝东坐，居于尊贵的席位；亚父范增朝南坐；刘邦朝北坐，屈居下座；张良朝西陪坐。

Narrator: King Xiang hosts a grand banquet. Xiang Yu and Xiang Bo occupy the honored seats facing east, while Fan Zeng sits facing south. Liu Bang, in a lower seat, faces north, accompanied by Zhang Liang sitting towards the west.

刘邦：(谦卑)参见将军！

Liu Bang: (Humbly) Greetings, General!

项羽：(盛气凌人)请坐！

Xiang Yu: (Domineering) Please have a seat!

刘邦：谢将军！

Liu Bang: Thank you, General!

刘邦：我和将军合力反秦，将军在黄河以北作战，我在黄河以南作战，但是我自己没有料到能先进入关中。虽然先入咸阳，只因运气好而已，但是我绝不敢称王。一定是有小人进献谗言，使我们之间产生了误会。

Liu Bang: General, you and I have united forces to attack the Qin regime. You fought in the north of the Yellow River, while I fought in the south. However, I never expected to enter Guanzhong first. Though I was fortunate to capture Xianyang, it was merely a stroke of luck. I would never dare to declare myself a king. There must be someone who slandered me, causing this misunderstanding between us.

项羽：是你的部下曹无伤向我进言，否则我不会误会你。

Xiang Yu: It was your subordinate, Cao Wushang, who misled me. Otherwise, I would not have misunderstood you.

旁白：范增多次向项羽使眼色，再三举起他佩戴的玉玦暗示项羽杀掉刘邦，项羽沉默着没有回应。范增愤而离席，出帐后找到项庄。

Narrator: Fan Zeng repeatedly signals to Xiang Yu. He raises the jade pendant he wears, hinting at killing Liu Bang. Xiang Yu remains silent, offering no response. Fan Zeng becomes irritated and leaves the banquet to seek out Xiang Zhuang.

范增：项王优柔寡断，不愿杀刘邦。现在你进去，假装祝酒，然后献上剑舞，伺机刺杀刘邦。否则，你们以后都将被他俘虏！

Fan Zeng: King Xiang is indecisive and unwilling to kill Liu Bang. Now, you go in there and pretend to offer a toast, followed by a sword dance. Take this opportunity to assassinate Liu Bang. If you fail, you will both be captured by him in the future!

项庄：是。

Xiang Zhuang: Understood!

旁白：项庄入场

Narrator: Xiang Zhuang enters the scene.

项庄：项王，请允许我舞剑以助兴！

Xiang Zhuang: King Xiang, may I have the honor of performing a sword dance to liven up the atmosphere?

项羽：好！

Xiang Yu：Very well!

旁白：项庄舞剑，剑锋直逼刘邦，可谓险象环生。项伯见情况危急，拔剑而出。

Narrator: Xiang Zhuang is performing the sword dance, with the blade pointing dangerously at Liu Bang. Sensing the critical situation, Xiang Bo swiftly draws his sword in response.

项伯：一人舞剑过于无聊，两人舞剑才有趣味。

Xiang Bo: It's more engaging to have two people perform the sword dance rather than one.

旁白：项伯张开双臂，像鸟儿张开翅膀那样用身体掩护刘邦，项庄无法刺杀沛公。

Narrator: Xiang Bo extends his arms like a bird spreading its wings, using his body to shield Liu Bang. Xiang Zhuang is unable to injure Liu Bang.

第三幕

Act 3

———

樊哙闯帐，卫护刘邦

Fan Kuai Breaks into the Banquet, Protecting Liu Bang

【人物】 项羽、刘邦、范增、樊哙、张良

【Characters】 Xiang Yu, Liu Bang, Fan Zeng, Fan Kuai, Zhang Liang

【场景】 鸿门宴会

【Scene】 Hongmen banquet

【剧本】

【Script】

旁白：张良见情形危急，急忙离席寻找樊哙。

Narrator: Zhang Liang realizes the gravity of the situation, swiftly leaves his seat, and hurries to find Fan Kuai.

张良：我们主公命悬一线，情况十分危急。项庄明着是在舞剑，其实是想刺杀主公。

Zhang Liang: Our lord's life is in imminent peril; the situation is extremely dangerous. Xiang Zhuang's swordplay is merely a facade, masking his true intention to assassinate our lord.

樊哙：（急切）情况如此危急，我将不惜性命以救主公！

Fan Kuai: (Urgently) The situation is dire, and I am prepared to risk my life to save our lord!

旁白：樊哙拿着剑，持着盾牌，闯进宴会。

Narrator: Fan Kuai takes his sword and shield and forcefully enters the banquet.

项羽：（见樊哙闯进来，大声呵斥）来者何人？

Xiang Yu :(Seeing Fan Kuai enter, sternly) Who is this?

樊哙：我是沛公的参乘樊哙。

Fan Kuai: I am Fan Kuai, in service of the Duke of Pei.

项羽：壮士！ 赐酒。

Xiang Yu: Brave warrior! Offer him a drink.

旁白：侍从递酒给樊哙，樊哙一饮而尽。

Narrator: A servant presents a drink to Fan Kuai, which he consumes in one gulp.

项羽：（环顾左右）再赐一条猪前腿。

Xiang Yu: (Looking around) Also give him a roasted pig's foreleg.

旁白： 侍从就给了樊哙一条未煮熟的猪前腿。樊哙把他的盾牌扣在地上，把猪腿放在盾牌上，拔出剑来切着吃。

Narrator: The servant hands Fan Kuai an undercooked pig's foreleg. Fan Kuai places his shield on the ground, lays the pig's foreleg on it, and draws his sword to cut and eat it.

项羽： 壮士！可否再来一杯？

Xiang Yu: Warrior! Would you like another cup of wine?

樊哙： 我连死都不惧，再喝一杯又何妨？秦王有虎狼一样的心肠，杀人唯恐不能杀尽，处罚唯恐不能用尽酷刑，所以天下人都反叛。怀王曾和诸将约定"先打败秦军进入咸阳的人封作关中王"。现在沛公先打败秦军进了咸阳，一丁点东西都不敢动用，封闭了宫室，军队退回霸上，等待大王到来。派遣将领把守函谷关的原因，是防备其他盗贼进入和意外发生。这样劳苦功高的人，没有得到赏赐，反而因小人谗言性命不保。这是延续已亡的秦朝的作为罢了。我以为大王不应该采取这种做法。

Fan Kuai: I do not fear death, let alone another cup of wine! The Qin Emperor was voracious and wolfish by nature, and he slaughtered the people without mercy, with the intent to exterminate them all. His punishments were cruel and excessive, driving the people to rebel against him. King Huai had made an agreement with the generals that "the one who defeats the Qin army and enters Xianyang first shall be titled the King of Guanzhong". Now, the Duke of Pei has defeated the Qin army and entered Xianyang, but he dares not utilize any resources. He has sealed the palace and withdrawn the army to

Bashang, patiently awaiting your arrival. Dispatching generals and soldiers to guard the Hangu Pass is to prevent other marauders from entering and to avoid unforeseen incidents. Yet, such tireless efforts go unrewarded, and instead, due to the schemes of petty individuals, his life is now in peril. This only perpetuates the practices of the deceased Qin Dynasty. I firmly believe that Your Majesty should not endorse such actions.

项羽:(无言以对)赐座。

Xiang Yu: (Speechless)Take a seat.

旁白:樊哙挨着张良坐下。刘邦起身,项羽叫住他。

Narrator: Fan Kuai sits beside Zhang Liang, while Liu Bang stands up, only to be stopped by Xiang Yu.

项羽:沛公何去?

Xiang Yu: Where are you headed?

刘邦:抱歉,我想如厕。

Liu Bang: My apologies, I need to visit the restroom.

旁白:樊哙随刘邦出帐。张良也紧跟其后,劝告刘邦尽快离开。

Narrator: Fan Kuai follows Liu Bang out of the tent; Zhang Liang also exits, advising Liu Bang to depart swiftly.

刘邦:我就这样不辞而别,是否有失礼数?

Liu Bang: Is it impolite to leave without bidding farewell?

樊哙:成大事者不拘小节。现在人家好比是菜刀和砧板,我们则好比是鱼和肉。主公还是尽快离开吧!

Fan Kuai: Those who achieve great things do not worry about trivial matters. Right now, they are like a kitchen knife and a chopping board, and we are like fish and meat. My lord should leave this place as soon as possible!

旁白：刘邦离开后，抄小路回到军营。张良带着刘邦留下的礼物入帐。

Narrator: Then Liu Bang leaves, and he takes a shortcut back to his military camp. Zhang Liang enters the tent, bringing the gifts left by Liu Bang.

张良：沛公不胜酒力，不能当面辞别，让我奉上白璧一双敬献大王，玉斗一双拜献亚父。

Zhang Liang: The Duke of Pei was too drunk to bid farewell in person. He asked me to give Your Majesty a pair of white jade as an offering and the General a pair of jade buckets as an offering.

项羽：沛公何在？

Xiang Yu: Where is he now?

张良：听说大王要责备他，他便独自离开，已经回到军营了。

Zhang Liang: He heard that Your Majesty intended to reprimand him, so he left on his own and returned to the military camp.

范增：（把玉斗扔在地上，悲愤）唉！夺项王天下的人一定是刘邦，我们都要被他俘虏了！

Fan Zeng: (Throwing the jade bucket on the ground, furiously) The man who exploited King Xiang's power must be Liu Bang, and we will be captured by him one day.

项羽：（尴尬）相信我，我总会杀了他！

Xiang Yu: (Awkwardly) Trust me that I will seize a chance to kill him in the end!

旁白：范增因不满项羽的优柔寡断而愤然离开。从此项羽一败再败，最后被汉军逼至乌江。项羽自刎。

Narrator: Fan Zeng storms off in anger, deeply dissatisfied with Xiang Yu's indecisiveness. As a consequence, Xiang Yu suffers repeated defeats and is ultimately cornered by the Han army at the Wujiang River. Overwhelmed by despair, Xiang Yu takes his own life by wielding his sword.

三、故事赏析 Story Analysis

《鸿门宴》是中国两千多年来脍炙人口的名篇。这个故事情节跌宕起伏，扣人心弦。在鸿门宴上，项羽盛气凌人又优柔寡断，刘邦能屈能伸又随机应变。鸿门宴是项羽、刘邦两大政治集团之间的一场激烈的斗争，双方领袖的性格在历史发展重要关头起到了重要的作用。最后，刘邦打败项羽，建立了西汉王朝。

"The Hongmen Feast" has been a celebrated masterpiece in Chinese history for over two millennia. There are gripping twists and turns as the narrative between the two unfolds, and it has long captivated the audience. During the banquet, Xiang Yu exhibited arrogance and indecisiveness whereas Liu Bang showed resilience and flexibility. The banquet serves as a battleground for two prominent political factions, Xiang Yu and Liu Bang, and their different personalities shape a pivotal moment in Chinese history. Ultimately, Liu Bang triumphs over Xiang Yu, and ushers in the Western Han Dynasty.

第二节
Section Two

桃园结义
The Peach Garden Oath

一、故事梗概 Synopsis

东汉末年，宦官当权，朝政腐败，人民生活非常困苦，黄巾军起义爆发了。太守刘焉四处张贴招募榜文，准备招兵买马，讨贼安民。榜文让志趣相投的刘备、关羽和张飞相识。在一个桃花绚烂的园子里，三人举酒对天盟誓，结拜为异姓兄弟。

In the declining years of the Eastern Han Dynasty, the corrupt rule of the eunuchs and the suffering of the people led to the Yellow Turban Uprising. Prefecture Liu Yan put out notices calling for volunteers to serve against the rebels and restore peace. Three kindred spirits, Liu Bei, Guan Yu, and Zhang Fei, were drawn to these notices. In a vibrant garden adorned with blossoming peach trees, they vowed their allegiance to the heavens with raised cups. The trio solemnly pledged to become sworn brothers despite their different surnames.

二、戏剧舞台 Theatre Stages

第一幕

Act 1

——

太守刘焉招募兵马, 刘张相识志趣相投

Prefecture Liu Yan Enlists Troops; Liu Bei and Zhang Fei Forge Camaraderie

【人物】 刘备、张飞

【**Characters**】 Liu Bei, Zhang Fei

【场景】 城中招募榜旁

【**Scene**】 In front of a notice displayed in the city

【剧本】

【**Script**】

旁白: 东汉末年, 宦官当道, 朝政腐败, 黄巾军起义爆发了。黄巾军直逼幽州, 太守刘焉四处张贴招募榜文, 准备招募兵马, 讨贼安民。

Narrator: In the twilight of the Eastern Han Dynasty, with the oppressive rule of eunuchs and a corrupt government, the flames of the Yellow Turban Uprising engulf the land. As the rebel forces advance towards Youzhou, Prefecture Liu Yan disseminates recruitment notices far and wide. He tries to amass an army capable of quelling the rebellion and restoring much-needed peace to the realm.

刘备:(看着榜文,叹息)唉——

Liu Bei: (Gazing at the notice, sighs) Ah ...

张飞:(站在刘备身后,声如巨雷)大丈夫不为国家出力,为何在此唉声长叹?

Zhang Fei: (Standing behind Liu Bei, his voice booming like thunder) Why does a true man sigh here instead of lending his strength to the nation?

刘备:(回头打量,心生敬仰)壮士所言极是。我看你身材魁梧,豹头环眼,一定不是平凡之人。请问尊姓大名?

Liu Bei: (Turning around, admiringly) You are absolutely right. I see that you have a robust figure with round eyes and well-formed forehead, and believe you are no ordinary person. May I ask for your honorable surname?

张飞:(拱手)不敢当,您过奖了。我姓张名飞,字翼德。世世代代居住在此,家里也有些基业。自己以卖酒卖肉为生,平常就爱结交天下豪杰。刚才看到你对着榜文叹息,所以才上前问问。

Zhang Fei: (Bows respectfully, with his palms pressed together in front of his chest and fingers extended upward) I am flattered, but I dare not accept your praise. I am surnamed Zhang, named Fei, with the courtesy name Yide. My family has resided here for generations, and we possess some land. I make a living by selling wine and meat, and I take pleasure in befriending heroes from all over the world. I noticed your sigh in front of the recruitment notice, so I came forward to inquire.

刘备:(回礼,谦恭状)我姓刘名备,字玄德,本是汉室宗亲,只是家道中落,沦落到以贩卖草鞋为生。最近听说黄巾军四处猖狂作乱,我虽然地位低下,但是也有心为国出力,只恨没有机会,所以叹息。

Liu Bei: (Returning the courtesy, modestly) My surname is Liu, my given name is Bei, and my courtesy name is Xuande. I am a distant relative of the Han imperial family. However, due to my family's decline, I have been forced to make a living by selling straw sandals. Recently, I heard about the rampant activities of the Yellow Turban rebels. Though I have a humble status, I yearn to contribute to the country. Unfortunately, I have not yet had the opportunity to serve the court, which is why you heard me sighing.

张飞：(激昂)我家产丰厚，可以变卖一些用作资助，来招募兵丁，一起报效朝廷。

Zhang Fei: (Passionately) My family holds considerable wealth that can be liquidated to support recruitment efforts and assist the court.

刘备：(大喜)这真是太好了。我们好好计划一下。

Liu Bei:(Joyfully) It sounds great. Let's make a good plan.

张飞：(爽快)好！我们到前面的酒家去，边喝边谈。

Zhang Fei:(Eagerly) Great! Let's go to the tavern ahead to drink and discuss our plans.

第二幕

Act 2

———

关羽入城为投军，巧遇刘张约结拜

Guan Yu Enters the City to Join the Army; Agreeing to Forge the Sworn Brotherhood with Liu Bei and Zhang Fei

【人物】 刘备、张飞、关羽

【**Characters**】 Liu Bei, Zhang Fei, Guan Yu

【场景】 城中酒家内

【Scene】 Inside a tavern in the city

【剧本】

【Script】

旁白：刘备和张飞感觉很是投缘，两人兴致勃勃地来到酒家。谈话间，只见一位大汉推着货车放在店前，径直进来。

Narrator: Liu Bei and Zhang Fei quickly bond with each other and arrive at a tavern, filled with enthusiasm. As they converse, their attention is drawn to a burly man pushing a cart outside the tavern, who then enters.

关羽：(高声)小二，快拿酒来，喝完我要赶紧去投军。

Guan Yu: (Loudly) Waiter, bring me some wine! After drinking, I must hurry to join the army.

刘备：(注视，心生敬仰)这位壮士，能否与我俩一起同桌饮酒？

Liu Bei: (Gazing, admiringly) Brave warrior, care to join us for a drink?

关羽：(耿直)这没什么不好啊。(起身来到刘备桌前)

Guan Yu: (Upright) Sounds good to me. (Standing up and joining Liu Bei's table)

刘备：壮士请坐。敢问尊姓大名？

Liu Bei: Please have a seat, hero! May I have your name?

关羽：我姓关名羽，字云长，是河东解良人。当年有豪强欺负百姓，我因为看不惯就把他给杀了，流落江湖已有五六年。听说太守正在招募兵士，特地前来投军。

Guan Yu: My surname is Guan, given name Yu, and courtesy name Yunchang. I am from Xieliang in Hedong. I have been wandering around for the past five or six years after killing a tyrant who oppressed the common people. I heard that the Prefecture is currently recruiting soldiers, so I come here to enlist.

刘备:(看了张飞一眼,再看向关羽)我们三人的想法不谋而合。

Liu Bei: (Glancing at Zhang Fei, then turning to Guan Yu) Our thoughts align perfectly, the three of us.

张飞:(高声)就是,就是,我们想到一块去了。

Zhang Fei: (Loudly) Exactly! We all have the same idea.

关羽:(高兴)真是太好了。

Guan Yu: (Joyfully) Fantastic.

张飞:(诚恳地)我家庄后有一处桃园,花开得正盛。明天我们三人在那里祭拜天地,结为生死兄弟,同心协力,共图大事。怎么样?

Zhang Fei: (Sincerely) On my estate, there's a peach garden with beautiful blossoms. Tomorrow, let's gather there to pay respect to heaven and earth and become sworn brothers. Together, we'll be united in purpose and strive for greatness. How does that sound?

刘备、关羽:(齐声)好,太好了。

Liu Bei, Guan Yun: (Simultaneously) Excellent! That sounds perfect!

第三幕

Act 3

———

刘关张桃园三结义

Liu, Guan and Zhang —Sworn Brothers in the Peach Garden

【人物】 刘备、关羽、张飞

【Characters】 Liu Bei, Guan Yu, Zhang Fei

【场景】 张飞庄后桃园

【Scene】 The Peach Garden behind Zhang Fei's estate

【剧本】

【Script】

旁白：第二天，张飞叫人杀猪宰羊，在桃园准备好祭品。刘备、关羽、张飞一同来到了桃园。

Narrator: On the following day, Zhang Fei instructs his servants to make preparations in the peach garden. Pigs and sheep are slaughtered, and offerings are carefully arranged. With everything in place, Liu Bei, Guan Yu, and Zhang Fei gather in the garden.

张飞:（庄重）结拜仪式开始。

Zhang Fei: (Solemnly) Let the initiation ceremony commence.

刘备、关羽、张飞:（跪地，齐念）刘备、关羽、张飞，虽为异姓，愿结为兄弟，同心协力，救困扶危，上报国家，下安黎庶。不求同年同月同日生，但愿同年同月同日死！皇天后土，实鉴此心，背义忘恩，天人共戮。

Liu Bei, Guan Yu, Zhang Fei: (Kneeling, reciting in unison) Liu Bei, Guan Yu, Zhang Fei, though our surnames may differ, we pledge to become sworn brothers; united in purpose, to aid the oppressed and assist the needy, to serve our country and bring peace to the people. We do not seek to share the same birthday, but we desire to share the same fate! May heaven and earth bear witness to our sincerity. If any of us should stray from our duty, let heaven and earth, as well as the people, be our judges.

张飞:(拉长音)礼成。(困惑)我们谁是大哥、二哥呢?

Zhang Fei: (Elongating his voice) The ceremony is complete. (Confused) So, who shall be the eldest brother and the second brother?

关羽:(深情)我们情同手足,就按年龄排。

Guan Yu: (Emotionally) Our bond is like that of siblings, so let's go by age.

刘备:(认真)按年龄,我是大哥,云长是二哥,翼德就是三弟了。

Liu Bei: (Earnestly) By age, I shall be the eldest brother; Yunchang will be the second brother; and Yide is the third.

关羽、张飞:(行礼)拜大哥。

Guan Yu, Zhang Fei: (Bowing) Salute to the eldest brother.

张飞:(再向关羽行礼):拜二哥。

Zhang Fei: (Bows to Guan Yu): Salute to the second brother.

刘备:(沉思)我们明日就去投军。大家准备使用什么兵器呢?

Liu Bei: (Contemplatively) Tomorrow, we shall join the army. What weapons do you plan to wield?

张飞:(急切高声)我要打造一支丈八蛇矛,直戳反贼心脏。

Zhang Fei: (Eagerly and loudly) I'll forge a serpent spear, eight feet long, to strike at the hearts of rebels.

关羽:(不甘示弱)我要打造一把八十二斤重的青龙偃月刀,手起刀落,像切瓜一样砍掉贼军脑袋。

Guan Yu: (Assertively) I'll forge a Qinglong Crescent Blade, weighing 41 kilos, to swiftly decapitate enemies like slicing melons.

刘备:(轻声)我准备两把宝剑,就叫双股剑,一样杀敌。

Liu Bei: (Softly) I am preparing two treasured swords named Shuanggu, using them to slay enemies.

张飞：好了，现在让我们开怀畅饮，明天一起去投军，建功立业。

Zhang Fei: Very well. Let's drink and enjoy ourselves. Tomorrow, we will join the army and make a distinguished career.

旁白：三人在桃园中痛饮起来。

Narrator: The three of them begin to drink heartily in the peach garden.

三、故事赏析 Story Analysis

故事中的人物形象饱满，表现了刘备的宽厚仁爱，关羽的义气为先，张飞的爽直粗豪。三人虽然有着迥然不同的性格脾气，但他们契若金兰，兄谦弟恭，互相关爱，互相帮助，共同成就了一番伟业。桃园结义的故事广为流传，成为朋友志同道合的代表，对后世有着很深的影响。很多人崇拜这三人，继而仿效起来，即志趣、性格等相近或互相投缘的人，通过一定的形式，结为兄弟般的关系，互相关心、互相帮助、互相照应。久而久之，这逐渐演变成一种具有人文色彩的礼仪习俗。

The story of "The Peach Garden Oath" vividly portrays the characters of Liu Bei, Guan Yu, and Zhang Fei, each with their own unique personality and strengths. Liu Bei is benevolent and kind; Guan Yu is loyal and brave; and Zhang Fei is straightforward and bold. Despite their contrasting personalities, they forge an unbreakable bond of brotherhood, demonstrating humility and respect for one another. They deeply care for and assist each other, united in their pursuit of a great cause. The story has resonated widely, serving as a representative of like-minded individuals. Its profound impact on future generations is undeniable. Many people admire and emulate the action of forming brotherly relationships with those who share similar values and virtues, cemented through sacred rituals. This practice fosters a life of mutual care, support, and consideration, gradually evolving into a kind of cherished cultural tradition.

第三节
Section Three

———

巧施连环计

The Chaining Schemes

一、故事梗概 Synopsis

东汉末年,奸臣当道,董卓专权。董卓骄横残暴,为非作歹,早有篡权之心,并且身边又有骁勇善战的吕布相助,朝中文武官员无计可施,朝廷危亡。王允为国分忧,巧施连环计,安排了美人计和离间计,计计相连,环环相扣,利用美女貂蝉离间了董卓与吕布之间的关系,使得二人反目成仇,最后利用吕布杀了董卓。

In the final years of the Eastern Han Dynasty, treacherous court minister Dong Zhuo held absolute power, ruling with arrogance and brutality. His wicked intentions of usurping the throne were further bolstered by the presence of his fierce and skilled subordinate, Lü Bu. Helpless against this formidable duo, the civil and military officials of the court saw the imperial government teetering on the edge of destruction. To safeguard the state, Wang Yun devised these clever and interconnected strategies, employing the Beauty Trap and the Discord Scheme. These intricate schemes were meticulously crafted, each step leading seamlessly into the next. Through the mesmerizing beauty Diao Chan, Wang Yun skillfully sowed seeds of discord between Dong Zhuo and Lü Bu, causing them to turn against one another. Ultimately, Wang Yun seized the opportunity to manipulate Lü Bu into assassinating Dong Zhuo.

二、戏剧舞台 Theatre Stages

第一幕

Act 1

———

王允妙定连环计

Wang Yun Prepares the Chaining Schemes

【人物】 王允、貂蝉

【Characters】 Wang Yun, Diao Chan

【场景】 王允府后院亭子内

【Scene】 Pavilion in the backyard of Wang Yun's residence

【剧本】

【Script】

旁白：王允下朝回府，想到董卓把持朝政，骄横残暴，夜不能寐。他来到后院，忽然听到有人在长吁短叹，发现竟是府中歌姬貂蝉，上前询问原因。

Narrator: One night, Wang Yun is unable to sleep due to his concerns over Dong Zhuo's tyrannical rule and control of the imperial court. He strolls into the backyard, hoping to clear his head. Suddenly, he hears someone sighing deeply. He finds Diao Chan there, one of the household singing girls. Wang Yun approaches her, eager to understand the cause of her distress.

王允：你深夜在此悲伤叹气,有什么心事吗?

Wang Yun: What are you sighing about out here in the darkness? What's troubling you?

貂蝉：近日我看大人您总是眉头紧锁,很焦虑的样子。我深受您的恩德,叹息自己不能做些什么为您分忧。

Diao Chan: I've noticed lately that my lord's brows have knitted in distress. I am grateful for your kindness and I am miserable on my lord's account. I wish I could do something to ease your concerns.

王允：如今奸臣当道,我是为国担忧。你一个小女子又能做些什么呢?

Wang Yun: With the current rises of treacherous officials, I worry for our nation. But what can a young woman like you do to help?

貂蝉：大人待我恩重如山,只要用得上小女子,我一定在所不辞。

Diao Chan: My lord, you've been so kind to me. Use your handmaid in any way; I will never shrink.

旁白：王允感动之余,突然计上心头。

Narrator: Touched by her words, Wang Yun suddenly conceived a plan.

王允：(向貂蝉跪拜)天下兴亡,全在你的手上。

Wang Yun: (Kneeling and bowing in front of Diao Chan) The fate of Han lays on your palm.

貂蝉：(大惊)大人快快请起,有什么事情您尽管吩咐就是。

Diao Chan: (Frightened) Oh, please, stand up, my lord. What is it that you need? I am here to serve you.

王允：如今奸臣董卓把持朝政，无恶不作，还想篡位，又有其义子吕布为虎作伥，越发猖狂。现在朝廷危亡，又没有什么好的办法，全靠你了。我听说二人皆为好色之徒，我想施以美人计，先将你献于吕布，再将你献于董卓；你再离间父子二人，使得他们内讧，再除之而后快。只是你要周旋于二人之间，危机重重，你可愿意？

Wang Yun: Right now, that wicked Dong Zhuo has all the power in the imperial court. He's doing all sorts of evil things and even planning to take the throne for himself. And to make matters worse, his foster son Lü Bu is right there, supporting him every step of the way. The court is in serious trouble, and we're running out of solutions. That's where you come in. I've heard that both of them are lechers, and I am going to use what I may call the "chaining schemes". I'll first present you to Lü Bu; and then, after you are betrothed, I will present you to Dong Zhuo. You'll then use your charms to create discord between them and make them turn against each other, and then put an end to the great evil. However, this plan entails great risks, as you will need to deal with them. Are you up for it?

貂蝉：(叩拜)小女子承蒙大人收养，待我如亲生女儿一般，无以为报。眼下能有机会为大人分忧解难，我定当全力以赴。

Diao Chan: (Kneeling) My lord, you've been like a father to me, taking me in and treating me with such kindness. I owe you everything. Now, I have a chance to repay your kindness and help you go through this difficult time. I'll give it everything I've got.

王允：真是委屈你了。

Wang Yun: Your sacrifice means the world to me.

103

第二幕

Act 2

———

王允献貂蝉于吕布

Wan Yun Presents Diao Chan to Lü Bu

【人物】 王允、貂蝉、吕布

【Characters】 Wan Yun, Diao Chan, Lü Bu

【场景】 王允府

【Scene】 Wang Yun's residence

【剧本】

【Script】

旁白：王允打造金冠秘密地送给吕布，吕布亲自到王允府上致谢。王允设宴。

Narrator: Wang Yun covertly commissions a golden crown and sends it as a gift to Lü Bu. Lü Bu pays a personal visit to Wang Yun's residence to express his gratitude. Wang Yun, in turn, arranges a banquet to entertain his guest.

王允：如今天下英雄，唯将军耳！敬将军一杯。

Wang Yun: Cheers to you, General, the most distinguished among the heroes of our time!

吕布：（大喜）承蒙大人错爱，干杯。

Lü Bu: （Delighted） I'm flattered. Cheers.

王允：（几杯过后，假装醉酒）老夫年事已高，实在不胜酒力，不如请我家小女前来侍奉将军喝酒。

Wang Yun: （Pretending to be tipsy after a few drinks） I'm not as young as I used to be, and I can't hold my liquor anymore. General, how about having my daughter join us and take care of you?

吕布:(喜悦)甚好。

Lü Bu: (Joyfully) Great.

旁白:貂蝉进,吕布见貂蝉貌美,忍不住一直盯着她看。

Narrator: Diao Chan enters, and Lü Bu finds himself unable to tear his gaze away from her exquisite beauty.

王允:这是我家小女貂蝉,目前还没有许配人家。将军不嫌弃的话,不如娶小女为妻?

Wang Yun: Allow me to introduce my daughter, Diao Chan. She is currently unmarried. If she pleases you, General, why not consider taking her as your wife?

吕布:司徒大人,此事甚好。只是不知小姐心意如何?

Lü Bu: Minister Wang, this is indeed a remarkable proposal. However, I wonder what the young lady thinks?

貂蝉:小女子久闻将军大名,若能侍奉将军,是我的荣幸。

Diao Chan: General, I have long known of your great reputation. It would be an honor for me to serve by your side.

王允:那就挑选良辰吉日,把你们的婚事定下来吧。

Wang Yun: Excellent! Let us choose an auspicious day to finalize the marriage arrangements.

吕布:谢谢司徒大人,我改日一定备下厚礼上门提亲。

Lü Bu: Thank you, Minister Wang. On another occasion, I will come bearing betrothal presents to formally propose to the lady.

第三幕

Act 3

——

王允再献貂蝉于董卓

Wang Yun Presents Diao Chan to Dong Zhuo

【人物】 王允、貂蝉、董卓

【Characters】 Wang Yun, Diao Chan, Dong Zhuo

【场景】 王允府

【Scene】 Wang Yun's residence

【剧本】

【Script】

旁白：王允在府上宴请董卓，貂蝉上前以歌舞助兴。董卓见貂蝉姿色绝美，不由得垂涎三尺。

Narrator: Wang Yun invites Dong Zhuo to a feast at his mansion. Diao Chan comes forward to sing and dance, adding to the festivities. Dong Zhuo is utterly captivated by Diao Chan's mesmerizing beauty. He finds himself consumed by desire for her.

董卓：这名女子是谁？

Dong Zhuo: Who is this woman?

王允：她是府中歌姬貂蝉。

Wang Yun: She is Diao Chan, one of the talented singers in my household.

董卓：真是神仙中人。

Dong Zhuo: What a fairy lady!

王允：(窃喜)太师若喜欢，可将貂蝉收入府中。

Wang Yun: (Secretly pleased) Grand Tutor, if you fancy Diao Chan, you are welcome to have her in your household.

董卓：(哈哈大笑)不知怎么感谢司徒呢。

Dong Zhuo: (Laughs heartily) I can't express my gratitude enough.

王允：今天就给您送到府上。

Wang Yun: I will arrange for her to be sent to your residence today.

旁白：吕布听说王允把貂蝉送给了董卓，赶去质问王允。

Narrator: Upon hearing that Wang Yun has given Diao Chan to Dong Zhuo, Lü Bu hurries to Wang Yun's residence to confront him.

吕布：（怒气冲冲）你把貂蝉许配给我，怎么又把她送给太师？真是岂有此理！

Lü Bu: (Enraged) You promised to betroth Diao Chan to me, so why did you give her to the Grand Tutor? This is unreasonable!

王允：你错怪老夫了。太师到府中，我禀告他说已将貂蝉许配给将军。太师要求带她回去与你成亲，我怎敢阻拦呢？

Wang Yun: You have misunderstood me. When the Grand Tutor visited my house, I informed him that Diao Chan had already been betrothed to you, General. However, the Grand Tutor requested to take her home and marry her to you. How could I dare to stand in his way?

第四幕

Act 4

———

貂蝉离间吕布与董卓

Diao Chan's Manipulations Cause Strife Between Lü Bu and Dong Zhuo

【人物】 貂蝉、吕布、董卓

【Characters】 Diao Chan, Lü Bu, Dong Zhuo

【场景】 凤仪亭

【Scene】 The Phoenix Pavilion

【剧本】

【Script】

旁白:吕布听说董卓已将貂蝉纳为小妾,十分气愤。吕布拜见董卓时,貂蝉在旁边以手指心,表明心迹,又以手指董卓。吕布见状心痛万分。貂蝉寻找机会约吕布在后院的凤仪亭见面。

Narrator: Upon learning that Dong Zhuo has taken Diao Chan as his concubine, Lü Bu becomes furious. During Lü Bu's visit to Dong Zhuo, Diao Chan stands beside Dong Zhuo. She gestures towards her heart and then towards Dong Zhuo, expressing her true feelings for Lü Bu. This deeply saddens Lü Bu. Diao Chan seeks an opportunity to meet Lü Bu at the Phoenix Pavilion in the backyard.

吕布:我们明明定好了婚约,你为何出尔反尔嫁给了别人,而且还是我的义父?

Lü Bu: We'd already made an agreement. Why did you break your promise and marry my foster father of all people?

貂蝉:(哭泣)我的心只在将军这里,奈何你义父横行霸道,偏偏要霸占我。我一小女子怎敢反抗?我已经对不起将军了,只想投池自尽,只是想到还没与将军告别,才勉强撑到今日。现在,我已心无所求,只要一死了之。

Diao Chan: (Weeping) My heart has always been yours, General. But your foster father is forceful and takes advantage of me. As a helpless woman, I couldn't fight back. I have already betrayed you, and all I want is to end my life. But I couldn't bear to part with you without saying goodbye, so I endured until today. Now, I have nothing left to live for and only seek death.

旁白:貂蝉假装投池,吕布阻拦并抱住她。

Narrator: Diao Chan pretends to jump into the pond, but Lü Bu grabs her and holds her tight.

吕布：你千万不能做傻事，是我没能保护好你。

Lü Bu: Don't be so foolish! It's my fault for not protecting you.

貂蝉：（仰慕）将军是威风八面的大英雄，为何要甘居人后？只要你愿意同你义父抗争，我一定跟你走。

Diao Chan: (Admiringly) General, you're a mighty hero. You shouldn't yield to your foster father like this. If you're willing to stand up against him, I'll be right there by your side.

吕布：（叹息）是啊，我为何要屈服，连心爱的女人都保护不了。

Lü Bu: (Sighs) You're right. Why should I submit and fail to protect the woman I love?

旁白：董卓在府中不见吕布和貂蝉，心中起疑，便在后院寻找，远远看到凤仪亭中这二人依偎在一起，怒火中烧。董卓拿起画戟刺向吕布，吕布见董卓要杀自己，拔腿就跑。

Narrator: Unable to find Lü Bu and Diao Chan in the mansion, Dong Zhuo grows suspicious. He goes to the backyard and searches for them. From a distance, he sees Lü Bu and Diao Chan embracing at the Phoenix Pavilion. He flies into a rage, grabs a long lance, and thrusts it at Lü Bu. Lü Bu, fearing for his life, quickly flees.

董卓：（生气）你好大的胆子，怎么敢与吕布私通！

Dong Zhuo: (Angrily) How dare you have an affair with Lü Bu!

貂蝉：（哭泣）奴婢冤屈呀。我在后院赏花，不想吕布突然出现。我看他居心不良，就准备投池自尽，却被他抱住。正在这时，太师赶来，我才得以脱身。我还是死了算了。

Diao Chan: (Crying) I have been wronged! I was simply enjoying the flowers in the backyard, and unexpectedly, Lü Bu appeared. I sensed his evil intentions and was ready to end my life by jumping into the pond. But he stopped me. It was at that moment that you ar-

rived, allowing me to escape. I'd rather die.

董卓: 好了,好了,都是吕布太可恶了。

Dong Zhuo: Fine, fine. Lü Bu is too despicable.

旁白:在貂蝉的离间之下,董卓与吕布二人心生嫌隙,从此交恶。

Narrator: Diao Chan's actions manipulate a rift between Dong Zhuo and Lü Bu, leading to their enmity.

第五幕

Act 5

———

王允施展计中计,吕布诛杀董卓

Wang Yun Executes the Chaining Schemes; Lü Bu Assassinates Dong Zhuo

【人物】 王允、吕布、董卓

【**Characters**】 Wang Yun, Lü Bu, Dong Zhuo

【场景】 王允府

【**Scene**】 Wang Yun's residence

【剧本】

【**Script**】

旁白:吕布痛恨董卓夺妻,整天郁郁寡欢,到王允府中诉说心中的苦闷。王允趁机再施一计,用言语刺激吕布,怂恿吕布诛杀董卓。

Narrator: Lü Bu, deeply resenting Dong Zhuo for taking his wife, is perpetually despondent. He goes to Wang Yun's residence to express his distress. Seizing the opportunity, Wang Yun employs another scheme, provoking Lü Bu with words and inciting him to assassinate Dong Zhuo.

王允：（长叹）太师食言，抢夺将军之妻，恐怕为天下人耻笑。其实，更多的是耻笑将军啊。可惜，将军英雄盖世，却要受到这样的侮辱。

Wang Yun:（Sighing）The Grand Tutor broke his promise and took your wife. His actions will bring disgrace upon him. But it is you, General, who will suffer the most from the ridicule. It is a shame that a heroic general like you has to put up with this humiliation.

吕布：（发怒，拍案而起）我发誓一定要杀了这个老贼，以报夺妻之仇。

Lü Bu:（Angry, slams the table）I swear I'm gonna take down that old wretch and get revenge for snatching my wife.

王允：（嘘声）将军不要讲了，免得引来灾祸。

Wang Yun:（Hushing）General, please be cautious with your words. We don't want to attract unnecessary trouble.

吕布：大丈夫立于天地之间，怎能甘居人下？我决定要杀了此贼。

Lü Bu: As a man of honor, how can I be enslaved? I've made up my mind to kill that scoundrel.

王允：（暗喜）将军若愿诛杀太师，其实也是匡扶汉室，就是朝廷的忠臣，定能留名青史。

Wang Yun:（Secretly delighted）General, if you are willing to assassinate the Grand Tutor, it will not only serve as retribution but also contribution to the restoration of the Han Dynasty. You will be remembered as a loyal minister in the pages of history.

吕布：好，愿听大人差遣。

Lü Bu: Very well, I am willing to carry out your orders.

111

旁白: 王允假传圣旨,宣董卓入朝,然后由吕布刺死了董卓。

Narrator: Wang Yun uses an imperial edict as a pretext to summon Dong Zhuo to the imperial court. It is there that Lü Bu stabs him to death.

三、故事赏析 Story Analysis

自古巾帼不让须眉。貂蝉是中国古代四大美人之一,有倾国倾城之貌。在朝廷危难之时,貂蝉愿意为国分忧,听从王允的计谋安排,先施美人计,利用自己的美貌迷惑董卓和吕布;再施离间计,挑拨二人之间的关系,使得他们反目成仇。两个计谋环环相扣,缺一不可,形成连环计,最后利用吕布诛杀了董卓。在这个故事中,貂蝉发挥了主要作用,没有她就不能除掉奸臣。

Throughout history, women have proven their ability to achieve great things. Diao Chan, one of the Four Beauties of ancient China, was no exception. She possessed not only extraordinary beauty, but also a deep sense of duty to her nation. When she learned of the crisis in the imperial court, Diao Chan willingly took on the burden of her people. She followed Wang Yun's strategic plans, using her beauty to captivate both Dong Zhuo and Lü Bu. She then sowed discord between them, turning them against each other. These two interconnected schemes formed an intricate trap that ultimately led to the downfall of Dong Zhuo at the hands of Lü Bu. Diao Chan's pivotal role in this narrative cannot be overstated. Without her, the removal of the treacherous court official would not have been possible.

三顾茅庐

Making Three Trips to Visit Zhuge Liang in His Thatched Cottage

一、故事梗概 Synopsis

东汉末年,群雄四起,天下大乱。曹操挟天子以令诸侯,逐渐统一了北方。孙权凭借父兄的基业,励精图治,雄踞东南。刘备为复兴汉室而四处奔走,招贤纳士,希望能够成就一番事业。听闻诸葛亮非常有才,刘备屈尊求贤,三去卧龙岗,邀请他辅佐自己。诸葛亮感激刘备的三顾之恩,提出了先取荆州和益州,形成与曹操、孙权三足鼎立之势,最后再光复汉室的计划。这就是著名的三顾茅庐的故事。

During the waning years of the Eastern Han Dynasty, chaos engulfed the land as warlords rose to power. Cao Cao, leveraging his influence over the emperor, gradually unified the northern territories. Sun Quan, capitalizing on his family's legacy, focused on governance and established his authority in the southeast. Meanwhile, Liu Bei embarked on a quest to revive the Han Dynasty, traversing far and wide in search of talented individuals to support his aspirations. Upon learning of Zhuge Liang's remarkable abilities, Liu Bei humbly undertook a journey, visiting Zhuge Liang's thatched cottage at Wolonggang three times to invite him to join the cause. Deeply grateful for Liu Bei's persistence, Zhuge Liang proposed a strategic approach. This plan involved capturing the regions of Jingzhou and Yizhou as the first steps, thereby establishing a trilateral power balance with Cao Cao and Sun Quan. Ultimately, the goal was to reclaim the Han Dynasty. This renowned tale is known as "making three trips to visit Zhuge Liang in his thatched cottage".

二、戏剧舞台 Theatre Stages

第一幕

Act 1

——

刘备第一次拜访诸葛亮

Liu Bei's First Visit to Zhuge Liang

【人物】 刘备、关羽、张飞、书童

【Characters】 Liu Bei, Guan Yu, Zhang Fei, Lad servants

【场景】 卧龙岗诸葛亮家

【Scene】 Zhuge Liang's farmstead in Wolonggang

【剧本】

【Script】

旁白:刘备在新野驻军,听说诸葛亮是一个可以与姜子牙、张良相提并论的人才,决定亲自前往隆中去拜会。刘备带着关羽和张飞一起来到诸葛亮的门前。

Narrator: After stationing his army in Xinye, Liu Bei hears of Zhuge Liang, a talent comparable to Jiang Ziya and Zhang Liang. Determined to meet him, Liu Bei personally embarks on a journey to Longzhong, accompanied by Guan Yu and Zhang Fei. They arrive at Zhuge Liang's doorstep.

刘备:我是刘备,特来拜会诸葛先生。

Liu Bei: I am Liu Bei, and I've come to call on the Master.

书童:(鞠躬)我家先生一早就出去了。

Lad servants: (Bowing) The Master left this morning early.

刘备:(失望)先生到哪里去了?

Liu Bei: (Disappointed) Where has he gone?

书童:他行踪不定,不知道去哪里了。

Lad servants: His whereabouts are uncertain. I do not know where he has gone.

刘备:那他什么时候回来呢?

Liu Bei: When will he return, then?

书童:时间不确定,有时三五天,有时十多天。

Lad servants: That is also uncertain. Perhaps in three or five days, perhaps in ten.

刘备:(惆怅)哦。

Liu Bei: (Sighs) Oh.

张飞:(急切地)既然不在,我们就回去吧。

Zhang Fei: (Anxiously) Since he's not here, let's go back.

刘备:还是等一等吧。

Liu Bei: Wait a little longer.

关羽:(劝说)还是先回去吧,等他回来再说。

Guan Yu: (Persuading) It would be better to go back now and wait for his return.

刘备：(叮嘱书童)如果先生回来，就说刘备曾前来拜访。(望着关羽和张飞)那我们就回去吧。

Liu Bei: (Instructing the lad servants) When the Master returns, tell him that Liu Bei has been here. (Looking at Guan Yu and Zhang Fei) Now, let's go back.

第二幕

Act 2

———

刘备风雪中二访诸葛亮

Liu Bei's Second Visit to Zhuge Liang in the Snowy and Windy Day

【人物】 刘备、关羽、张飞、诸葛均

【Characters】 Liu Bei, Guan Yu, Zhang Fei, Zhuge Jun

【场景】 卧龙岗诸葛亮家

【Scene】 Zhuge Liang's farmstead in Wolonggang

【剧本】

【Script】

旁白：过了一段时间，已经进入寒冬。刘备听说诸葛亮回去了，就准备再次拜访。

Narrator: Some time has passed since their return to Xinye, and winter has descended upon the land. During this time, Liu Bei receives news of Zhuge Liang's return and prepares for yet another visit.

刘备：(高兴)卧龙先生回来了，两位贤弟随我前去拜访。

Liu Bei: (Joyfully) Mr. Wolong has returned. My dear brothers, accompany me to pay him another visit.

张飞:（不乐意）不就是个山野村夫,哥哥何必亲自去? 派人把他叫来吧。

Zhang Fei: (Reluctantly) Brother, why must you go personally looking for this villager? Send someone to summon him.

刘备:（责备）卧龙先生是当世的大贤,怎能随便召唤? 你们随我一起去。

Liu Bei: (Reproaching) Mr. Wolong is the greatest sage of our time. How can I summon him? Just come with me.

旁白:走了几里路后,寒风刮得更猛烈了,天空中下起了鹅毛大雪。

Narrator: They walk a few miles. The bitter wind blows even stronger, and the heavy snow begins to fly.

张飞:这天寒地冻的,我们大老远地跑去见一个无用之人,不如回去避一避大雪吧。

Zhang Fei: It's freezing out here and the ground is frozen! Yet we've come all this way to meet someone useless. Let's get back and take shelter from the snow.

刘备:（生气）我就是要让卧龙先生知道我们的诚意。你如果怕冷,就自己回去吧。

Liu Bei: (Angrily) I just want to prove our sincerity to Mr. Wolong, but if you fear the cold, you can go back.

张飞:（嘀咕）我死都不怕,怎么会怕冷呢?

Zhang Fei: (Muttering) I do not fear death. Do you think I care about the cold?

刘备:（严肃）那就不要多言,跟上就是了。再走一会我们也就到了。

Liu Bei: (Seriously) Then stop complaining and keep up. We'll arrive soon if we walk a little farther.

刘备:(来到门前,敲门进入)卧龙先生,我终于见到您了。

Liu Bei: (Arriving at the door, knocking, and entering) Mr. Wolong, I finally met you.

诸葛均:(不好意思)我是他弟弟,我哥哥昨天和朋友出去了。

Zhuge Jun: (Sorry) I'm his younger brother. My brother went out with his friend yesterday.

刘备:(失望)我来了两次都没见到卧龙先生,真是遗憾。那我改日再来拜会。

Liu Bei: (Disappointed) I have visited Mr. Wolong's dwelling twice, but to my great regret I fail to see him. I will come another day.

第三幕

Act 3

———

刘备第三次拜访诸葛亮

Liu Bei's Third Visit to Zhuge Liang

【人物】 刘备、关羽、张飞、诸葛亮、书童

【Characters】 Liu Bei, Guan Yu, Zhang Fei, Zhuge Liang, Lad Servants

【场景】 卧龙岗诸葛亮家

【Scene】 Zhuge Liang's farmstead in Wolonggang

【剧本】

【Script】

旁白:光阴荏苒,已是早春时节。刘备打算第三次去拜访诸葛亮。

Narrator: Time slips away, and it is now early spring. Liu Bei plans to pay Zhuge Liang a third visit.

关羽：哥哥都去过两次了，这礼节也太重了吧。说不定他是虚有其名，所以不敢见您呢。

Guan Yu: Brother, you've made two visits already; it seems like an excessive and grand show of deference. I doubt his supposed fame is deceptive; perhaps he lacks the courage to face scrutiny.

张飞：不劳哥哥了，我用麻绳把他绑来。

Zhang Fei: Don't bother, brother. I'll bring him here with a hemp rope.

刘备：(责备)你们难道不知道周文王拜访姜子牙的故事吗？周文王都如此礼贤下士。你们怎能这么无礼呢？不要多言，快随我一起去。

Liu Bei: (Rebuking) Have you forgotten the noble example of King Wen's visit to Jiang Ziya? He could display such reverence towards a wise man. How dare you show such disrespect? Let's not waste words, just come with me.

刘备：(敲门，见到书童)请通报卧龙先生，刘备专程拜访。

Liu Bei: (Knocking at the door and seeing the lad servants) Please inform Mr. Wolong that Liu Bei wishes to call on him.

书童：先生今天在家，只是还在睡午觉呢。

Lad Servants: The Master is at home, but he's taking a nap.

刘备：既然这样，那就等他醒了再通报吧。

Liu Bei: In that case, do not announce my visit till he wakes up.

张飞：(等了一阵，大怒)我去房后放一把火，看他起来不起来。

Zhang Fei: (After waiting for a while, getting angry) I wanna go to the back of the house and set a fire, and see if that will rouse him.

刘备：（呵斥）不得无礼。

Liu Bei:（Scolding）Don't be rude.

诸葛亮：（睡醒后吟诵）大梦谁先觉？平生我自知。草堂春睡足，窗外日迟迟。

Zhuge Liang:（Reciting after waking up）Who first awakens from a splendid dream? It has been my understanding all along. In the thatched cottage, I find ample rest in spring, with daylight lingering outside the window.

书童：先生，刘皇叔拜访，已等候多时了。

Lad Servants: Master, the Uncle of the Emperor Xian is here. He has been waiting for a long time.

诸葛亮：快快请他进来。

Zhuge Liang: Hurry, invite him in.

第四幕

Act 4

————

三分天下隆中对

The Longzhong Plan: Divide the Empire into Three Parts

【人物】 诸葛亮、刘备、书童

【**Characters**】 Zhuge Liang, Liu Bei, Lad Servants

【场景】 卧龙岗诸葛亮家

【**Scene**】 Zhuge Liang's farmstead in Wolonggang

【剧本】

【**Script**】

旁白: 书童恭敬地请刘备进屋,刘备终于见到了诸葛亮。关羽和张飞在屋外等候。

Narrator: The lad servants respectfully invite Liu Bei inside. Liu Bei meets Zhuge Liang eventually. Guan Yu and Zhang Fei wait outside.

诸葛亮:(行礼)拜见将军。

Zhuge Liang: (Bowing) Greetings, General.

刘备:(高兴)我一直仰慕先生大才,之前已来过两次都没见到您,今天有幸拜会。

Liu Bei: (Delighted) I have long admired your great talent. I have come to visit you twice, without success. Today, I am fortunate to have this meeting.

诸葛亮: 不敢当。请问有何指教?

Zhuge Liang: You flatter me. May I ask what brings you here?

刘备: 眼下朝廷奸佞当道,百姓受难,我想光复汉室,知道您有雄才大略,特请赐教。

Liu Bei: Currently, the crafty sycophants hold sway, and the people are suffering. I wish to restore the Han Dynasty. I know you possess great wisdom and foresight. Will you instruct me?

诸葛亮:(推辞)我一介书生,恐怕难当大任。

Zhuge Liang: (Declining) I am but a humble scholar and may not be suitable for such a significant undertaking.

刘备: 请先生以天下苍生为念,不要推辞。

Liu Bei: I conjure you, Master, to remember the inhabitants of the world and bestow instructions upon me.

诸葛亮: 那我就勉为其难,姑且直言了。今日天下大乱,豪杰并起。曹操拥有百万雄兵,挟天子以令诸侯,势不可挡。孙权占据江东,励精图治,雄踞东南。眼下唯有荆州和益州,将军要重点考

虑。(书童拿上地图)将军请看,这是西川五十四州的地图,先占领荆州站稳脚跟,再攻打西川建立基业。这样形成三足鼎立之势,最后再统一天下。您觉得如何?

Zhuge Liang: In that case, I will reluctantly accept. Let me speak frankly. One after another, bold individuals have emerged across the empire, causing significant upheaval and turmoil. Now Cao Cao wields immense power, commanding a formidable army of a million soldiers and exercising control over the feudal lords through his influence at the court. You cannot think of opposing him. Then Sun Quan occupies Jiangdong, striving to govern, and dominating the southeast. Currently, only Jingzhou and Yizhou remain. General, you should focus on these regions. (The lad servants bring a map) General, as you can see, there are fifty-four counties in Xichuan. You should first conquer Jingzhou to establish a stronghold, and then focus on Xichuan to lay the foundation of our dominance. This will create a tripartite balance. Once the time is ripe, you can lay your plans for the attainment of the whole empire. What do you think?

刘备:(鞠躬)先生一席话,让我茅塞顿开。如您不嫌弃,请您出山辅佐我。

Liu Bei: (Bowing) Your words have enlightened me, Master. I hope you will not dislike me and leave this retreat to help me.

诸葛亮:(回礼)承蒙厚爱,我愿效犬马之劳。

Zhuge Liang: (Bowing back) I am honored by your trust. I will render what trifling service I can.

三、故事赏析 Story Analysis

三顾茅庐的故事广为流传。刘备求贤若渴,为了请诸葛亮出山,他屈尊三次前往卧龙岗。诸葛亮满腹经纶,有经天纬地之才,隐居卧龙岗，未出茅庐，已知三分天下。诸葛亮出山以后，给刘备出谋划策，联吴抗曹，三分天下，为建立蜀汉政权发挥了重要作用。这个故事告诉我们人才的重要性，必须尊重人才，充分发挥人才的作用。

The tale of Liu Bei's three visits to Zhuge Liang's retreat is widely known. Motivated by his lofty aspirations and the urgent need of capable advisors, Liu Bei humbly visited Wolonggang on three occasions, hoping to recruit Zhuge Liang. Zhuge Liang, renowned for his wisdom and strategic acumen, chose a reclusive life at Wolonggang. Even before leaving his retreat, Zhuge Liang anticipated the division of the empire into three factions. Upon joining Liu Bei, he played a crucial role in advising him, forming an alliance with Sun Quan to oppose Cao Cao, and establishing the Shu Han regime. This story underscores the importance of recognizing and harnessing the talents of exceptional individuals.

青梅煮酒论英雄

Discuss Heroes When Drinking in a Plum Garden

一、故事梗概 Synopsis

刘备与吕布交战失利,迫于形势,无奈暂时归附曹操。曹操大破吕布后班师回朝,邀汉献帝田猎,借机试探百官对自己的态度,他欺君的举动激起了皇帝和百官的愤怒。汉献帝秘密赐给国舅董承袍带,内藏血字诏书,要求董承讨伐曹操。刘备也加入了讨曹的联盟,但是为防备事情败露,就每日种菜浇园以掩人耳目。一日,曹操派人请刘备到丞相府上一叙,刘备提心吊胆地来到相府,引出了关于"当今天下谁是英雄"的讨论。

After Liu Bei's defeat in the battle against Lü Bu, he was forced to temporarily submit to Cao Cao due to the circumstances. Following decisive victory over Lü Bu, Cao Cao returned to the capital and invited Emperor Xian for a hunting expedition. This was an opportunity for Cao Cao to gauge the loyalty of his officials. However, Cao Cao's actions, which appeared to be disrespectful towards the emperor, provoked the anger of both the emperor and the officials. In secret, Emperor Xian presented a robe to Dong Cheng, his maternal uncle, with an edict written in blood, instructing him to lead a campaign against Cao Cao. Liu Bei also joined the alliance against Cao Cao, but to avoid arousing suspicion, he disguised his activities by tending to his garden and cultivating vegetables as a farmer. One day, Cao Cao sent an invitation to Liu Bei, who, filled with apprehension, went to the prime minister's residence. Unknowingly, this led to a discussion about the current heroes in the world.

二、戏剧舞台 Theatre Stages

第一幕

Act 1

———

董承秘受衣带诏，皇叔义愤要除曹

Dong Cheng Receives a Secret Command in the Palace; Liu Bei's Fury to Eliminate Cao Cao

【人物】 董承、刘备

【Characters】 Dong Cheng, Liu Bei

【场景】 刘备府

【Scene】 Liu Bei's residence

【剧本】

【Script】

旁白:国舅董承收到了皇帝的衣带血诏,准备讨伐曹操,为聚集力量,前来寻求刘备的支持。

Narrator: State Uncle Dong Cheng has received the emperor's edict written in blood and sewn into a girdle. He intends to launch a campaign against Cao Cao. In order to gather support, he visits Liu Bei to seek his assistance.

刘备:国舅深夜来访,一定是有重大的事情吧。

Liu Bei: It must be something unusually important that has brought the State Uncle here tonight.

董承:如果白天来访,恐怕引起曹操的怀疑。前几天田猎之时,你的二弟关云长要杀曹操,你却摇头制止,不知道是何意?

Dong Cheng: If I had rode forth in daylight, Cao Cao might have suspected something. A few days ago, during the hunting expedition, your second brother, Guan Yunchang, attempted to kill Cao Cao. Yet, you shook your head and stopped him. I wonder what your intentions were.

刘备:(大吃一惊)你是怎么知道的?

Liu Bei: (Startled) How did you know?

董承:不用紧张,别人都不知道,只有我是无意发现的。

Dong Cheng: No need to be alarmed. Nobody else noticed, and I just learned about it by accident.

刘备:我二弟看到曹操有欺君的行为,忍不住就有些怒气。

Liu Bei: My brother witnessed Cao Cao's act of disrespect towards our emperor, and he couldn't help but feel angry.

董承:皇上给了我衣带血诏,要求讨伐曹操。

Dong Cheng: His Majesty has given me a secret edict written in blood, ordering a campaign against Cao Cao.

刘备:国舅既然是奉诏讨贼,我当效犬马之劳。只是事关重大,必须谨慎从事,不可操之过急。

Liu Bei: State Uncle, since you have been entrusted with the mission to defeat the traitor, I will do my utmost to serve. However, considering the gravity of the situation, we must proceed with caution and not act hastily.

董承:感谢皇叔深明大义,我们从长计议。

Dong Cheng: Thanks for your profound understanding and righteousness. Let's deliberate on our plan from a long-term perspective.

第二幕
Act 2

———

曹操派人相请,刘备忐忑赴约
Cao Cao's Invitation and Liu Bei's Anxious Attendance

【人物】 刘备、张辽、许褚

【**Characters**】 Liu Bei, Zhang Liao, Xu Zhu

【场景】 刘备家的后院

【**Scene**】 The backyard of Liu Bei's residence

【剧本】

【**Script**】

旁白:为防止秘密泄露而遭曹操谋害,刘备韬光养晦,每天不出门,就在后院浇花种菜。这一天,关羽和张飞外出,刘备正在后院浇菜,曹操突然派张辽、许褚来请刘备到曹操府上一叙。

Narrator: In order to prevent the secret from being released and to avoid any plots by Cao Cao, Liu Bei chooses to keep a low profile. He rarely leaves his home and spends his days in the backyard tending to his plants. On this particular day, Guan Yu and Zhang Fei are out, and Liu Bei is watering the garden when suddenly, Cao Cao sends Zhang Liao and Xu Zhu to invite Liu Bei to a meeting at Cao Cao's palace.

张辽、许褚：(拱手行礼)刘使君，丞相差遣我们来请您到府上一叙。

Zhang Liao and Xu Zhu: (Bowing respectfully) Lord Liu, the Prime Minister has sent us to invite you to his mansion for a meeting.

刘备：(起身，手提水桶，吃惊)这么仓促，丞相有什么要紧事吗?

Liu Bei: (Standing up, carrying a water bucket, surprised) This is quite sudden. Does the Prime Minister have an urgent matter?

张辽、许褚：这个我们也不太清楚，只说请您过去。

Zhang Liao and Xu Zhu: We are not entirely sure, but we were simply instructed to invite you.

刘备：(思索片刻)二位将军请稍等片刻，我收拾一下就来。

Liu Bei: (Pausing to think) Generals, please wait a moment. Let me tidy up and I will join you shortly.

第三幕

Act 3

———

青梅煮酒论英雄

Heroes Discussed Over Hot Rice Wine and Green Plums

【人物】 刘备、曹操、侍者

【Characters】 Liu Bei, Cao Cao, Servants

【场景】 相府后院

【Scene】 The backyard of the Prime Minister's Residence

【剧本】

【Script】

旁白：刘备随侍从入相府见曹操，表面强作镇定，实际上心中忐忑不已。

Narrator: Liu Bei follows a servant into Cao's Residence. His heart pounds in his chest as he tries to appear composed.

曹操：(大笑，嘲讽意味)你在家做大事啊！

Cao Cao: (Laughing sarcastically) That is a big business you have in hand at home.

刘备：(面如土色)我……

Liu Bei: (Pale-faced) Well, I ...

曹操：(认真)玄德学习种菜很不容易，正好今日无事，特地请你来赏景聊天。

Cao Cao: (Seriously) Xuande, the growth of vegetables that you are trying to learn is very difficult. Since we have some free time today, I thought we could enjoy the scenery and chat.

刘备：(稍微放心，谦恭)种菜浇园只是消遣罢了。今日丞相难得有此雅兴，刘备自当奉陪。

Liu Bei: (Slightly relieved and humble) It is only a solace. Since the Prime Minister has this rare interest today, I am honored to accompany you.

曹操：(得意状)刚才见到枝头梅子青青，我忽然想起去年征讨张绣时，路上缺水，将士都很渴。我心生一计，拿马鞭虚指前方说(以手指前方)："前面有片梅子林。"将士听说后，口中生唾液，也就不渴了。今天再见到梅树，不可不欣赏一番(骄傲)，又恰巧酒刚煮热，所以邀请使君到小亭相聚。

Cao Cao: (Jaunty) I happened to notice the green plums on trees just now, and they reminded me of a ruse I used during the campaign against Zhang Xiu last year. Our soldiers were suffering from thirst. Suddenly I lifted my whip, and pointing at something in the distance (pointing his hand forward), I said, "There's a plum grove up ahead." Upon hearing that, the soldiers' mouths started watering, and they no longer felt thirsty. Today, seeing the plum trees again, I couldn't help but appreciate them (proudly). I ordered the servants to heat some rice wine and sent them to invite you to share the view and the wine at this small spring pavilion.

刘备:(心神方定)那实在是一个妙计!

Liu Bei: (Calming down) What an ingenious stratagem!

曹操:酒已煮好,玄德,请!

Cao Cao: The rice wine is ready. Xuan De, please!

刘备:丞相请!

Liu Bei: Please!

侍者:(立于曹操身后,惊喜)丞相请看,刚才天上乌云密布,现在好像有一条龙。

Servants: (Standing behind Cao Cao, pleasantly surprised) Prime Minister, could you please take a look! The sky was full of dark clouds just a moment ago, and now it appears like a dragon in the sky.

曹操:哦?(眯眼远眺,点头再转向刘备)你听说过龙的种种变化吗?

Cao Cao: Oh? (Squinting and nodding, then turning to Liu Bei) Have you heard about the various transformations of a dragon?

刘备:(挺直远眺)我见识浅薄,不太清楚。

Liu Bei: (Gazing into the distance) My knowledge is limited, so I'm not very familiar with it.

曹操：龙能大能小,能升腾,能隐匿;大则腾云驾雾,小则隐藏不见;升则飞腾于宇宙间,隐则潜伏于波涛内。如今正是晚春,龙随时节变化,好比人得志而纵横四海,可比为当世的英雄。玄德经常在外游历,一定知道当世英雄,请你说说看。(伸手邀请)

Cao Cao: A dragon can assume any size, can rise in glory or hide from sight. Mounting, it can soar to the empyrean; subsiding, it lurks in the uttermost depths of the ocean. This is the late spring season, and the dragon chooses different time for its transformations like a person realizing his/her own desires and overrunning the world. You have traveled all lakes and rivers and must have known who are the heroes of the present day. Why don't you share your thoughts? (Extending his right hand as an invitation)

刘备：(谦逊)我见识浅薄,怎么认得出谁是英雄?

Liu Bei: (Modestly) I am just a common dullard, how can I know such things?

曹操：(仰面笑)你太谦虚了。

Cao Cao: (Throwing up his head and laugh) Don't be so modest.

刘备：(局促)备蒙受您的恩德才有机会在朝廷做个官,要让我说天下的英雄,实在不清楚。

Liu Bei: (Abashed) It is thanks to your kindness that I have the opportunity to serve in the Court. As for knowing the heroes of the world, I'm afraid I'm not very clear.

曹操：就算没见过面,也应该听说过他们的名头。

Cao Cao: You may not have met them, but you may have heard their names.

刘备：(小心翼翼)淮南袁术,士兵粮草都充足,他算得上英雄。

Liu Bei: (Cautiously) Yuan Shu of the South of River Huai, with his strong army and abundant resources, is he one?

曹操:(哂笑)活死人而已,我早晚要活捉他。

Cao Cao: (Sneering) A rotting skeleton in a graveyard. I shall put him out of the way shortly.

刘备:(思索)河北袁绍,出身名门贵族,门下有很多忠诚的老臣,如今占据冀州,部下能人极多,肯定是英雄了。

Liu Bei: (Pondering) Yuan Shao in Hebei, born into a prestigious family, has many loyal and sophisticated ministers. He currently holds control over Jizhou and has a multitude of talented subordinates. He must be a hero.

曹操:(轻蔑)袁绍表面厉害,实际是个胆小鬼,做事优柔寡断,真要干大事反而缩手缩脚,见到小利益就不要命,不算英雄。

Cao Cao: (Disdainfully) A bully, but a coward. He is fond of grandiose schemes, but is devoid of decisions. He makes for great things but grudges the necessary sacrifice. He loses sight of everything else in view of a little present advantage. He does not qualify as a hero.

刘备:有个人号称是"八俊"之一,在全国都有好名声,刘景升可算个英雄?

Liu Bei: There is a person known as one of the "Eight Paragons", who has a good reputation throughout the country. Can Liu Jingsheng be considered a hero?

曹操:(不以为意)刘表徒有虚名,不是英雄。(挥手)

Cao Cao: (Unconcerned) He is a mere semblance, a man of vain reputation. No, not him. (Waving his hand)

刘备:(赞扬,竖拇指)有一个人血气方刚,年纪轻轻就统领江东,孙伯符真是个英雄!

Liu Bei: (Praising, giving a thumbs-up) There is a man full of energy who commands Jiangdong at such a young age. Sun Bofu is truly a hero!

曹操:(肯定)孙策凭借的是他父亲的基业和名声,不算真英雄。

Cao Cao: (Affirming) Sun Ce relies on his father's legacy and reputation, so he cannot be considered a true hero.

刘备:(急切)益州的刘璋,可算英雄?

Liu Bei: (Eagerly) How about Liu Zhang in Yizhou? Is he a hero?

曹操:刘璋虽是皇室一员,现在不过是一条看门狗,怎么配称英雄?

Cao Cao: Though he is a member of the reigning family, he is nothing more than a watch dog. How could you make a hero of him?

刘备:(试探)那张绣、张鲁、韩遂这些人怎么样?

Liu Bei: (Tentatively) What about Zhang Xiu, Zhang Lu and Han Sui?

曹操:(鼓掌大笑)全是平庸小人,不值一提!

Cao Cao: (Clapping and laughing) Paltry people like them are not worth mentioning!

刘备:(思虑片刻)除此之外,我实在是不知道了。

Liu Bei: (Contemplating for a moment) With these exceptions, I really know none.

曹操:(感慨)真英雄,胸怀大志,腹有良谋,能包藏宇宙的奥秘,有吞吐天地的气概。

Cao Cao: (Reflectively) Now heroes are the ones who cherish lofty designs and have plans to achieve them. They have all-embracing schemes, and the whole world is at their mercy.

刘备:(放下酒杯,拿起筷子准备夹菜,望向曹操)那到底谁能称得上英雄呢?

Liu Bei: (Setting down his wine cup, picking up his chopsticks to take food, looking at Cao Cao) So, who can truly be called a hero then?

曹操:(用手指向刘备,又指向自己)如今天下的英雄,只有你和我两个罢了！

Cao Cao: (Pointing his finger first at Liu Bei and then at himself) The only two heroes in the world are you and I.

旁白：刘备听到这里，心中大吃一惊，手中拿着的筷子竟然落到地上。就在此时，只听"轰隆"一声，雷电大作。在雷声的掩饰下，他从容地捡起筷子。

Narrator: Liu Bei gasps as he hears this, and his chopsticks rattle to the floor. At that very moment, thunder crackles in the sky. Hidden by the sound of thunder, he calmly picks up his chopsticks.

曹操：(怀疑地)嗯？

Cao Cao: (Suspiciously) Huh?

刘备：(起身，从容地捡起筷子放在桌上)没想到这雷声这么厉害，把我吓了一跳。

Liu Bei: (Rising and calmly placing the chopsticks on the table) I didn't expect the thunder to be so loud. It startled me.

曹操：(笑)大丈夫还怕打雷吗？

Cao Cao: (Laughing) Shouldn't a great man be afraid of the thunder?

刘备：(淡定)孔圣人听到刮风打雷也会变脸色，何况是我？

Liu Bei: (Calmly) The Confucius paled at a sudden peal of thunder and fierce gust of wind. Why should one not fear?

侍者：丞相，是否再热一坛酒？

Servants: Prime Minister, should we heat another pitcher of wine?

曹操：好，今日青梅煮酒论英雄，我们要喝个痛快。

Cao Cao: Very well. Let's have a good drink today and discuss more about heroes.

三、故事赏析 Story Analysis

刘备受邀加入了董承的讨曹阵营，为避人耳目就闭门不出。曹操对刘备心存疑虑，所以准备考验他一下。刘备心中发虚，处处小心应对。刘备担心曹操把他当作对手，怕曹操把他当作英雄。否则，别说刘备要实现自己的政治抱负，恐怕连人头都会不保。于是在曹操追问他天下英雄有谁时，他假装糊涂，处处设防，用其他人物来搪塞，比如袁术、袁绍、刘表等人。这些提名都被曹操寥寥数语一一驳回。最后曹操直指天下英雄唯有"你""我"，刘备吓得筷子都拿不住了。此时空中忽传惊雷，刘备借机掩盖自己的心虚，曹操也信以为真，对刘备打消疑虑，放松警惕。此后刘备成为曹操大敌，也才出现了后来三足鼎立的局面。

Liu Bei was invited to join Dong Cheng's anti-Cao faction, so he stayed indoors, avoiding public attention. Cao Cao had suspicions about Liu Bei and decided to test him. Liu Bei was anxious and handled every situation with caution. He feared that Cao Cao would see him as a rival or a hero. If that were the case, Liu Bei would not only fail to achieve his political ambitions but also be in danger. When Cao Cao asked him about the heroes in the world, Liu Bei pretended to be confused and used other figures like Yuan Shu, Yuan Shao, and Liu Biao as diversions. However, Cao Cao dismissed each of them with concise and pointed remarks. Finally, Cao Cao directly stated that they were the only two heroes in the world, leaving Liu Bei startled and unable to hold his chopsticks. Just then, thunder roared from the sky, and Liu Bei used it as an opportunity to conceal his unease. Cao Cao believed him, dispelled his doubts, and lowered his guard. Liu Bei's caution would serve him well in the future, leading to his eventual rise to power and the emergence of the Three Kingdoms.

空城计

The Empty City Stratagem

一、故事梗概 Synopsis

　　三国时期,诸葛亮因错用马谡而失掉战略要地——街亭,魏将司马懿乘势引十五万大军向诸葛亮所在的西城蜂拥而来。当时,诸葛亮身边没有大将,只有一班文官,在万般无奈之时设下了"空城计"。

In the era of the Three Kingdoms, Zhuge Liang suffered a setback when he misjudged Ma Su, leading to the loss of the strategically vital stronghold Jieting. Seizing this opportunity, Sima Yi, a general from the Wei Kingdom, swiftly mobilized an army of 150,000 soldiers and marched towards the West City where Zhuge Liang was stationed. With no experienced generals at his side, Zhuge Liang was compelled to employ the "Empty City Stratagem" as the last resort to deceive Sima Yi.

二、戏剧舞台 Theatre Stages

第一幕

Act 1

马谡大意失街亭

Ma Su's Negligence Results in the Loss of Jieting

【人物】 诸葛亮、马谡、王平、探子

【Characters】 Zhuge Liang, Ma Su, Wang Ping, Scouts

【场景】 祁山军营大帐

【Scene】 The Main Tent in Qishan Military Camp

【剧本】

【Script】

旁白：诸葛亮率军讨伐魏国，司马懿受命迎战，街亭成为双方争夺的咽喉要地。

Narrator: Zhuge Liang leads troops to battle against the Wei Kingdom, while Sima Yi is tasked by the Wei monarch to engage the enemy in combat. The Battle of Jieting becomes a pivotal battlefield contested by both sides.

探子：（匆匆进帐）报丞相，司马懿带领十五万大军，正向我方赶来。

Scouts:（Hurriedly entering the tent）Prime Minister, Sima Yi is leading an army of 150,000 troops and heading towards us.

诸葛亮：（紧张）司马懿领军前来，必定会先攻占街亭。街亭是我们的咽喉要道，事关重大，谁愿领兵镇守街亭？

Zhuge Liang:（Seems nervous）Sima Yi is coming with his army, and he will likely target Jieting first. Jieting is a crucial strategic point for us, and the situation is grave. Who is willing to lead the troops and defend Jieting?

马谡：(急切地)末将愿往。

Ma Su: (Eagerly) I'm willing to go.

诸葛亮：(沉吟)你虽然熟读兵书，但这个地方没有城池可以固守，我担心你守不住。

Zhuge Liang: (Contemplating) Although you are well-versed in military strategies, Jieting lacks fortified walls, and I am concerned about your ability to hold it.

马谡：(激昂，大声)军中无戏言，我愿立下军令状。

Ma Su: (Passionately, loudly) There is no room for jests in the army. I am willing to make a solemn oath to fulfill my duty.

诸葛亮：我派王平做你的副将，助你一臂之力。王平听令。

Zhuge Liang: I will appoint Wang Ping as your deputy general to support you. Wang Ping, listen to my order.

王平：末将在。

Wang Ping: Yes, Prime Minister.

诸葛亮：我知道你一向谨慎，但这次要更加小心。在街亭的要道安营扎寨，司马懿的兵马就不能轻易攻进去了。

Zhuge Liang: I know you are always cautious, but this time you must be even more careful. Pitch your camp at the strategic pass of Jieting, making it difficult for Sima Yi's forces to launch a direct attack.

王平：听从丞相安排。

Wang Ping: Yes, I will follow the Prime Minister's instructions.

马谡：(喃喃自语)我熟读兵书，丞相真是多虑了。

Ma Su: (Muttering to himself) I am well-versed in military stra-tegies. The Prime Minister is overly cautious.

旁白：马谡和王平领兵到街亭，马谡不听王平建议，执意要在山上驻扎，结果被司马懿大军团团围住，最后狼狈逃窜，街亭丢失。

Narrator: Ma Su and Wang Ping lead the troops to Jieting. Despite Wang Ping's advice, Ma Su insists on pitching their camp on the mountaintop. This decision proves disastrous as Sima Yi's overwhelming forces surround them, leaving them trapped. In a desperate attempt to flee, they are ultimately forced to abandon Jieting, resulting in its loss.

第二幕

Act 2

———

诸葛亮大摆空城计

Zhuge Liang Implements the Empty City Stratagem

【人物】 诸葛亮、文官、士兵、探子

【Characters】 Zhuge Liang, Civil Officials, Soldiers, Scouts

【场景】 西城城门

【Scene】 The Gate of West City

【剧本】

【Script】

旁白:司马懿攻占街亭之后,率领大军直奔诸葛亮在西城的驻地。西城之中没有一员大将,只有两千多名士兵和一些文官,形势危急。

Narrator: Having captured Jieting, Sima Yi marches his sizable army directly towards Zhuge Liang's stronghold in West City. Inside the city, there is a scarcity of notable generals, with only a few thousand soldiers and a handful of civil officials. The situation becomes incredibly precarious.

探子:(惊慌)丞相,大事不好了! 司马懿率军杀过来了。

Scouts: (Panicked) Prime Minister, things are not good! Sima

Yi is leading his troops and coming this way to attack us.

文官：（害怕）这可怎么办呢？力量太悬殊了，我们赶快逃吧！

Civil Officials:（Fearful）What should we do? We are too weak to win. We'd better leave here as soon as possible.

诸葛亮：（淡定）不要慌。（沉思之后）传令：把所有的战旗都藏起来；士兵们待在原地，如果有私自走动以及大声喧哗的，立即斩首。

Zhuge Liang :（Calmly）Don't panic. （After contemplation）Send out my order: Hide all the war flags, and soldiers remain in their positions. Anyone who acts independently or causes a disturbance will be executed on the spot.

士兵：得令。

Soldiers: Understood.

诸葛亮：（微笑）吩咐下去，把四个城门统统打开，每个城门内安排二十名士兵装扮成老百姓，洒水扫街。

Zhuge Liang :（Smiling）Give this command: Open all four city gates. Inside each gate, assign 20 soldiers disguised as ordinary civilians to sprinkle water and sweep the streets.

士兵：（吃惊）啊？

Soldiers: （Astonished）Shall we?

诸葛亮：（成竹在胸）不用怕，我自有妙计退敌。

Zhuge Liang: （Confidently）Do not be afraid. I have a brilliant plan to repel the enemy.

旁白：诸葛亮披上道服，戴上高高的帽子，领着两个小书童，带上一把古琴，登上城楼，凭栏坐下，燃起香，然后悠然地弹起琴来。

Narrator: Zhuge Liang dressed himself in a Taoist robe, donned a tall hat, accompanied by two young attendants, and carried a *guqin*. He appeared in the tower on the gate, sat down behind the railing, lit incense, and began to play the instrument leisurely.

第三幕

Act 3

———

司马懿中计慌撤退

The Trap Leading to Sima Yi's Hasty Retreat

【人物】 诸葛亮、司马懿、司马昭、文官、士兵

【Characters】 Zhuge Liang, Sima Yi, Sima Zhao, Civil Officials, Soldiers

【场景】 西城城门

【Scene】 The Gate of West City

【剧本】

【Script】

旁白:司马懿的先锋部队抵达城下,看到城门打开,不敢贸然进攻,急忙向司马懿报告。司马懿来到城下,看到诸葛亮在城楼上弹琴。

Narrator: Sima Yi's vanguard troops reach the city gate and observe it standing open. Uncertain about launching an immediate attack, they swiftly report the situation to Sima Yi. Sima Yi personally arrives at the gate and is confronted with a bewildering sight: Zhuge Liang, seated in the gate tower, calmly playing the *guqin*.

司马懿:(疑惑,继而坚定)命令全军快快撤退。

Sima Yi: (Puzzled, then determined) Order the entire army to retreat quickly.

司马昭:父亲,我看诸葛亮是没有兵马,才故弄玄虚做出这个

样子的。我们应当乘机杀进去,为什么要撤兵呢?

Sima Zhao: Father, I believe Zhuge Liang has no troops, and he is simply using this false illusion. We should seize the opportunity and enter the city. Why are we withdrawing?

司马懿:诸葛亮一生谨慎,从来都不会冒险行事,今日却打开城门,一定有埋伏。我军如果贸然进城,必定会中埋伏。你还年轻,不懂其中的厉害。不要再说了,赶快撤退。(于是各路兵马撤退而去。)

Sima Yi: Zhuge Liang is always cautious and never takes risks. Today, he opens the city gate, which means there must be an ambush. If our army rashly enters the city, we will fall into the trap. You are still young and do not understand the severity of the situation. Now, say no more and retreat immediately. (The troops then retreated.)

诸葛亮:哈哈,司马懿果真中计了。

Zhuge Liang: (Laughing) Sima Yi fell right into the trap.

文官:(佩服)丞相英明! 只是下官实在不解,司马懿是魏国名将,为什么见到了丞相,就立即撤退了呢?

Civil officials:(Impressed) Prime Minister, you are so brilliant! However, I am still puzzled. Sima Yi is a renowned general of Wei. Why did he immediately retreat upon seeing you?

诸葛亮:司马懿知道我一向小心谨慎,从来不会冒险。由于他生性多疑,当他看到我们城门打开,一定会怀疑我们设有伏兵,所以才会退兵。如果当时仓皇撤退,必定会被他们擒获。这也是不得已的办法。现在我们必须赶快退回汉中。

Zhuge Liang: Sima Yi knows that I am always cautious and never take risks. Due to his suspicious nature, when he saw our city gate open, he would doubt that we had set up an ambush. That's why he retreated. If we had hastily retreated at that moment, we would have been captured by them. It was a last resort. Now we must quickly return to Hanzhong.

第四幕
Act 4

———

诸葛亮挥泪斩马谡
Zhuge Liang's Tearful Execution of Ma Su

【人物】 诸葛亮、马谡、蒋琬

【**Characters**】 Zhuge Liang, Ma Su, Jiang Wan

【场景】 汉中军营大帐

【**Scene**】 The military camp in Hanzhong

【剧本】

【**Script**】

旁白:诸葛亮使用空城计吓退司马懿后,赶紧率军退回汉中。丢失街亭的马谡向诸葛亮请罪。

Narrator: Zhuge Liang uses the empty city stratagem to repel Sima Yi successfully, and promptly leads troops back to Hanzhong. Ma Su, who lost Jieting, begs Zhuge Liang for forgiveness.

马谡:(双手反绑,跪地)请丞相治罪。

Ma Su: (Hands bound behind, kneeling) Prime Minister, please punish me.

诸葛亮:(愤怒)你自幼熟读兵书,我才把守卫街亭的重任交付给你。现在街亭丢失,损兵折将,都是你的罪过。来人,推出去斩了。

Zhuge Liang: (Angrily) You have studied military books since childhood, and I entrusted you with the important task of guarding Jieting. Now Jieting is lost, with losses in both troops and commanders. This is all your fault. Take him away and behead him.

蒋琬:(求情)丞相息怒,请刀下留人。目前正是用人之际,请让他将功赎罪。

Jiang Wan: Prime Minister, please calm down. Spare his life. It is currently the time when talents are needed. Let him redeem himself through good deeds.

诸葛亮：我和马谡情同兄弟，但是治军必须从严。（大哭，自责）先帝曾对我说过，马谡言过其实，不可大用，现在果然应验了。这都是我的过失啊。

Zhuge Liang: Ma Su and I are as close as brothers, but military discipline must be strict. (Crying, self-blame) The late emperor once warned me about Ma Su's tendency to exaggerate and not be relied upon heavily. Now, it has come true. It's all my fault.

旁白：马谡被推出去斩首。

Narrator: Ma Su is pushed out and beheaded.

三、故事赏析 Story Analysis

"空城计"是《三国演义》中非常精彩的一个片段，展现了诸葛亮临危不乱的超凡智慧，最终化险为夷。在司马懿大军压城、形势危急的情况下，诸葛亮利用司马懿生性多疑的性格特点，成功诱使司马懿做出错误判断。同时，空城计也表现了马谡不顾实际情况、只会纸上谈兵的形象和诸葛亮勇于担当的形象。

"The Empty City Stratagem" is a remarkable story in the *Three Kingdoms Romance*. It demonstrates Zhuge Liang's extraordinary wisdom and his knack for turning danger into safety. Faced with the imminent threat of Sima Yi's advancing army, Zhuge Liang skillfully exploits Sima Yi's inherent suspicion to create a false impression, leading Sima Yi to make a critical misjudgment. This story also highlights Ma Su's inclination to engage in theoretical discussions without considering practical circumstances. Moreover, it showcases Zhuge Liang's willingness to take responsibility for his actions.

第五章
Chapter Five

两汉三国成语典故戏剧悦读

Theatrical Delights: Idioms from the Western Han, Eastern Han, and Three Kingdoms

第一节
Section One

—

将计就计

Beating Someone at Their Own Game

一、故事梗概 Synopsis

赤壁之战前，曹操所带的北方军队不习水战，就任命荆州降将蔡瑁、张允为水师都督训练军队。由于这二人熟悉水战，周瑜把他们看作战争胜败的关键，一直想除掉他们，却一时难以得手。蒋干是曹操手下的谋士，他因曾与周瑜同窗数载，要求去做说客劝降周瑜。周瑜闻讯就已猜出蒋干来意，便将计就计，摆下"群英会"，诱导他盗走假的曹军水师都督蔡瑁、张允二人的"投降书"，利用曹操的猜疑致使曹操错杀了二将。

Before the Battle of Chibi, Cao Cao's soldiers were mostly from the dry plains of the north and did not know how to fight effectually on water. So, Cao Cao appointed Cai Mao and Zhang Yun, former generals of Jingzhou who had surrendered, as naval commanders to train the troops. Zhou Yu recognized their expertise in naval warfare and considered them crucial to the outcome of the battle. He therefore aimed to eliminate them, but encountered obstacles in achieving his goal. Jiang Gan, a counselor under Cao Cao and Zhou Yu's childhood companion, offered to mediate and persuade Zhou Yu to surrender. Sensing Jiang Gan's true motives, Zhou Yu devised a cunning plan. He orchestrated a "Meeting of Heroes" and tricked Jiang Gan into stealing a forged letter of surrender from Cao Cao's naval commanders, Cai Mao and Zhang Yun. Taking advantage of Cao Cao's suspicions, Zhou Yu's scheme caused Cao Cao to mistakenly execute the two generals.

二、戏剧舞台 Theatre Stages

第一幕
Act 1

———

蒋干自荐劝降周瑜
Jiang Gan Volunteers to Persuade Zhou Yu to Surrender

【人物】 曹操、蔡瑁、张允、蒋干

【Characters】 Cao Cao, Cai Mao, Zhang Yun, Jiang Gan

【场景】 曹操营帐

【Scene】 Cao Cao's camp

【剧本】

【Script】

旁白:周瑜虽然在三江口挫败曹军,但发现曹操的军队由熟悉水战的蔡瑁和张允负责,担心长期下去曹军将锐不可当,认为要破曹军首要的是除掉这两人。曹操在三江口战败后,加强军队训练,准备再战周瑜。

Narrator: Although Zhou Yu defeated Cao Cao's army at the Battle of Chibi, he knows that Cai Mao and Zhang Yun, who are thoroughly experienced in naval warfare, pose a threat. He fears that if they continue to lead Cao Cao's forces, Cao Cao's army would become unbeatable. Zhou Yu believes that eliminating these two is crucial to defeating Cao Cao. Cao Cao, on the other hand, is not giving up. After his defeat, he has intensified training and is preparing for a rematch against Zhou Yu.

曹操:前几日三江口之战我们失利,挫了锐气。大家说我们应当怎么办?

Cao Cao: The other day we lost a battle, and the soldiers were greatly dispirited. What can be done?

蔡瑁:禀报主公,荆州的部队虽然熟悉水战,但已经很久没有实战了,北方的军队又不熟悉水上作战,才导致了失败。我们加强训练,战斗能力就会大大提升,到时打败敌人将易如反掌。

Cai Mao: My lord, the Jingzhou marines are indeed skilled in naval warfare, but they haven't had actual combat experience for a while. As for the soldiers from the north, they have no experience of naval warfare whatsoever. That's why we failed. We need to train and drill them extensively. Once they are proficient, victory will come easily.

张允:确实如此,目前首要的就是提高军队的水战能力。

Zhang Yun: Indeed, the most important thing is to improve our troops' ability in water warfare.

蒋干:我和周瑜从小是同窗好友,愿意凭借这三寸不烂之舌,劝说周瑜投降。

Jiang Gan: When I was young, Zhou Yu and I were fellow students and pledged friends. I will go over and convince him to surrender with my silver tongue.

曹操：你有把握吗？

Cao Cao: Are you sure about this?

蒋干：丞相放心，我去劝降，必定成功。

Jiang Gan: Don't worry, Prime Minister. I will go and persuade him, and I'm confident that I will succeed.

第二幕

Act 2

———

周瑜群英会蒋干

Zhou Yu Gathers Heroes to Meet Jiang Gan

【人物】 周瑜、蒋干、太史慈、将领

【Characters】 Zhou Yu, Jiang Gan, Taishi Ci, Generals

【场景】 周瑜营帐

【Scene】 Zhou Yu's camp

【剧本】

【Script】

旁白：周瑜正在帐中议事，听到蒋干来访，就已经猜到他的来意，心中已有主意，吩咐属下按计行事。

Narrator: Zhou Yu is in his tent, presiding over a council, when he receives word of Jiang Gan's visit. Sensing the intention behind his arrival, Zhou Yu devises a plan and discreetly shares instructions with his subordinates.

蒋干：公瑾别来无恙？

Jiang Gan: I hope you have been well since our last meeting.

周瑜：子翼辛苦了。你远道而来，莫非是要做说客吗？

Zhou Yu: You have endured hardship on your journey. Could it be that you have come here as a mediator?

蒋干：（故作愕然）我今天是来叙旧的，你怎么怀疑我是做说客呢？

Jiang Gan: (Pretending to be stunned) I came to visit you for the sake of old times. Why do you suspect me of being a mediator?

周瑜：（笑）我虽然不够聪明，但也能猜到一二。

Zhou Yu: (Smiling) Though I am not smart enough, I can still make some guesses.

蒋干：既然这样，我就告辞了。

Jiang Gan: As you choose to treat your old friend like this, I think I will take my leave.

周瑜：（笑而挽其臂）我只是担心你做曹操的说客，既然没有这事，何必早早离开呢？今天我们好好叙叙旧，也让你结识一下江东的英雄才俊。传令，设宴。

Zhou Yu: (Smiling and holding Jiang Gan's arm) I thought you might be here to persuade me on behalf of Cao Cao. Since that's not the case, why rush to leave? Let's take the opportunity to reminisce about the past and let me introduce you to the heroes of Jiangdong. Now, spread the word and prepare a feast to welcome my old friend.

旁白：周瑜设宴款待蒋干，传令悉召江东英杰与蒋干相见。文官武将各穿锦衣，帐下偏裨将校都披银铠，分两行而入。大摆宴席，奏军中得胜之乐，轮换行酒。

Narrator: Zhou Yu hosts a grand banquet to entertain Jiang Gan. He summons the heroes and talented individuals of Jiangdong to gather. Both civil and military officials dress in their finest attire. The military officers are adorned in shining silver armor, and the staff enter in two lines. Jiang Gan is introduced to everyone present. A lavish feast is laid out, and while they feast, the musicians play songs of victory and the wine circulates merrily.

周瑜:（对众将士）子翼是我的同窗好友,虽然是从江北过来的,却不是曹操的说客,大家不要有什么疑虑。（解下佩剑交给太史慈）今天由你做监酒,宴会之上只是交流朋友感情,如果有谁提及双方打仗之事的,可就地斩杀。

Zhou Yu: (To the generals) Jiang Gan is a good old friend and classmate of mine. Even though he comes from the North, he is not here as an envoy of Cao Cao. You have no reason to worry. (Removes his commanding sword and hands it to Taishi Ci) Today, you will be the master of the feast. Our gathering is solely for friendship and cama-raderie. If anyone dares to bring up the topic of war between two sides, just slay him.

太史慈:得令。

Taishi Ci: Understood.

蒋干:（惊愕）这……

Jiang Gan: (Surprised) But ...

周瑜:我自从领军以来,滴酒不饮。今天见到了老朋友,一醉方休。

Zhou Yu: Ever since I took command, I tasted no drop of wine, but today, with an old friend by my side, I am going to drink freely.

蒋干:(尴尬)好的,我们一醉方休。

Jiang Gan: (Awkwardly) Alright, let's drink till all's blue.

周瑜:(自豪)你看我的将士是否雄壮,我的粮草是否充足?

Zhou Yu: (Proudly) Do you find my soldiers full of power and grandeur? And do you think I have an ample supply of provisions?

蒋干:兵精粮足,名不虚传!

Jiang Gan：Your troops are mighty and your supplies ample; their fame is not unfounded!

周瑜:(佯醉大笑)回想我们上学之时,可不敢指望能有今天。

Zhou Yu：(Pretending to be quite intoxicated, laughing) Back when we were classmates, I never looked forward to a day like this.

蒋干:以公瑾的高才,实不为过!

Jiang Gan：For a genius like you, it's nothing extraordinary.

周瑜:(执蒋干手)假使苏秦等人复出,口似悬河,舌如利刃,也不能打动我的心。

Zhou Yu: (Seizing Jiang Gan's hand) Even if renowned orators like Su Qin were to reappear, with words flowing like mighty rivers and tongues as sharp as swords, they could not sway someone like me.

蒋干:确实。

Jiang Gan: Indeed.

周瑜:在座的都是江东的英雄豪杰,今天的盛会,我看就叫"群英会"。

Zhou Yu：Those present here are all the best and bravest of the land of the south; one might call this the "Meeting of Heroes".

153

第三幕

Act 3

———

周瑜用计诓骗，蒋干深信不疑

Zhou Yu Lures Jiang Gan into a Ruse

【人物】 周瑜、蒋干、军士

【Characters】 Zhou Yu, Jiang Gan, Soldiers

【场景】 周瑜营帐

【Scene】 Zhou Yu's tent

【剧本】

【Script】

旁白：周瑜假装大醉，邀请蒋干同房共寝，继续叙旧。二更时分，蒋干听到周瑜鼾声阵阵，偷偷起身来到桌前，看到上面有往来的书信，其中一封的封面上写着"蔡瑁 张允 谨封"。蒋干大吃一惊，打开一看竟然写着蔡瑁、张允二人策划投降的事情。正在此时，周瑜假装翻身，蒋干急忙把书信藏在衣服里，也上床假装睡着了。

Narrator: Zhou Yu pretends to be heavily intoxicated and invites Jiang Gan to share a room. They continue their conversation from earlier, and later Zhou Yu falls asleep. In the middle of the night, Jiang Gan hears Zhou Yu's loud snoring and quietly gets up. He approaches the table and discovers a pile of letters, including one with the inscription "Sealed by Cai Mao and Zhang Yun". Jiang Gan is greatly startled when he realizes that the letter reveals their plan to surrender. Just as this happens, Zhou Yu pretends to turn over in bed. Jiang Gan hurriedly conceals the letter in his clothes and returns to bed, pretending to be asleep.

周瑜:(含糊不清)子翼,我在数日之内,叫你看到曹操的首级。

Zhou Yu:(Muttering) Ziyi, I am going to let you see Cao Cao's head in a day or two.

蒋干:(勉强应之)嗯……

Jiang Gan:(Reluctantly responding) Uh ...

周瑜:子翼,且住!……叫你看曹贼之首!……

Zhou Yu: Wait a few days; you will see Cao Cao's head.

旁白:将近四更,只听得有人悄悄入帐。

Narrator:It is close to the fourth watch when someone quietly enters the tent.

军士:有紧要之事禀报,请都督醒一醒。

Soldiers: We have an urgent matter to report. Commander-in-Chief, please wake up.

周瑜:(假装刚睡醒,吃惊)床上睡着的是什么人?

Zhou Yu:(Pretending to awaken, surprised) Who is this on the bed?

军士:都督您请蒋干抵足而眠,怎么自己忘记了?

Soldiers: Do you not remember, Commander-in-Chief? You asked Jiang Gan to stay the night with you.

周瑜:(假装懊悔)我平时从来没有喝醉过,昨晚竟然喝醉了,不知道有没有胡言乱语。你有什么事情禀报?

Zhou Yu:(Feigning regret) I rarely get drunk, but last night I had too much. Perhaps I said many things I ought not. What do you have to report?

军士:江北有人到了。

Soldiers: Someone has arrived from the north.

周瑜:(低喝)小声点!

Zhou Yu:(Scolding in a low voice) Speak lower!

周瑜:(低呼)子翼？子翼？（蒋干假装睡着。周瑜走到帐外，蒋干起身偷听。）

Zhou Yu:(Calling in low voice) Ziyi, Ziyi. (Jiang Gan pretends to be sound asleep. Zhou Yu creeps out of the tent, while Jiang Gan listens with all his ears.)

军士:报告都督，蔡、张二位将军派人传话："近期难以得手，还在等待时机。"

Soldiers: Reporting to the Commander-in-Chief, Generals Cai Mao and Zhang Yun have sent a message: "It is difficult to achieve our goals in the near future. We are still waiting for the right opportunity."

旁白:周瑜入帐，又呼唤"子翼"。蒋干只是不应，蒙头假睡。周瑜见蒋干睡着，也就解衣就寝了。蒋干知道周瑜是非常精明的人，天亮后如果发现书信不见了，必定会找到并杀害偷信者。睡至五更，蒋干呼唤"公瑾"，见周瑜还睡着，就偷偷溜出营帐，准备逃回去。

Narrator:Zhou Yu reenters the tent, calling out for "Ziyi". Jiang Gan remains unresponsive, pretending to sleep soundly. Seeing Jiang Gan asleep, Zhou Yu undresses and goes to bed. Jiang Gan knows that Zhou Yu is meticulous. If Zhou Yu finds that the letter has disappeared in the morning, he will certainly find and kill the offender. So Jiang Gan lies there until near daylight and then calls "Gongjin". Getting no reply, he rises and slips out of the tent, preparing to escape to his home.

周瑜:(窃喜)我一直担心蔡瑁、张允，这二人是我们的劲敌。这次蒋干偷盗假的投降书回去，这二人必定会被曹操杀害，我再也不用担心了。

Zhou Yu: (Secretly pleased) I have always been concerned about Cai Mao and Zhang Yun. These two are formidable adversaries. Now that Jiang Gan has stolen the fake surrender letter, they will surely be executed by Cao Cao. I no longer have to worry.

第四幕

Act 4

———

曹操中计怒杀蔡张

Cao Cao Falls into the Trap and Furiously Executes Cai Mao and Zhang Yun

【人物】 曹操、蒋干、蔡瑁、张允、众将士

【Characters】 Cao Cao, Jiang Gan, Cai Mao, Zhang Yun, Generals

【场景】 曹操营帐

【Scene】 Cao Cao's camp

【剧本】

【Script】

旁白：蒋干偷了假信后连夜逃回曹营，向曹操汇报。

Narrator：Jiang Gan steals the forged letter, and flees back to Cao Cao's camp overnight to report.

曹操：子翼回来了，事情办得怎么样？

Cao Cao: Ziyi, you are back. How did things go?

蒋干：周瑜比较固执，高傲，不是言语能够打动的。

Jiang Gan: Zhou Yu is obstinate and truly high-minded. Nothing that I could say moved him in the least.

曹操：劝降的事情没有办成，恐怕还反被他嘲笑一番。

Cao Cao: So, the persuasion didn't work. I'm afraid he'll mock you for it.

蒋干：虽然没能劝降周瑜，我却打探到一件重要的事情，正要向丞相禀报。（将盗来的书信取出，呈给曹操。）

Jiang Gan：Well, although I did not persuade Zhou Yu successfully, I discovered something important. I was about to report it to you, Prime Minister.（Takes out the stolen letter and presents it to Cao Cao.）

曹操：（读完书信，大怒）传唤蔡瑁、张允。

Cao Cao:（After reading the letter, furious）Summon Cai Mao and Zhang Yun.

蔡瑁、张允：参见丞相。

Cai Mao, Zhang Yun: Present, Prime Minister.

曹操：我命令你们明天进攻周瑜。

Cao Cao: I order both of you to attack Zhou Yu tomorrow.

蔡瑁、张允：军队操练还不够熟练，不可贸然进攻。

Cai Mao, Zhang Yun: But the soldiers are not yet sufficiently trained. It's not advisable to launch a hasty attack.

曹操：（斥责）等军队操练熟练，恐怕我的脑袋早不在了。来人，将此二人拖出去斩了。

Cao Cao :（Rebuking）The soldiers will be well enough trained when you have sent my head to Zhou Yu, eh? Now, bring those two out and behead them.

旁白：蔡、张二人被拖出去斩首，不一会，他们的头颅献到帐下。

Narrator：Cai Mao and Zhang Yun were dragged out and beheaded. A short time later, their heads are presented in the tent.

曹操：（看到头颅，突然醒悟）我中计了。

Cao Cao:（Seeing the heads, suddenly realizing）I've been tricked.

三、故事赏析 Story Analysis

这个故事描写了赤壁大战前夕，曹操和周瑜双方各自施展手段，探听对方的虚实，企图引诱对方上当。特别是周瑜和蒋干抵足而眠，却都假装睡着，其中有多次偷偷起床再假睡的情节，并有轻声呼唤对方的细节，生动刻画了周瑜和蒋干的人物形象和性格特点，也描绘了一幅复杂斗争中尔虞我诈的情景。

This story depicts the events on the eve of the Battle of Chibi, where both Cao Cao and Zhou Yu employed various tactics to gather intelligence and deceive each other. The focus of the story is on the scene where Zhou Yu and Jiang Gan sleep together but pretend to be asleep. This scene is repeated many times, with both of them secretly getting up and then feigning sleep, calling each other's names in hushed voices. The story vividly portrays the characters and traits of Zhou Yu and Jiang Gan, as well as the atmosphere of cunning and deceit in the intricate struggle.

草船借箭

Borrowing Arrows with Thatched Boats

一、故事梗概 Synopsis

曹操率领百万大军南下,弱小的孙权和刘备结盟抵曹,双方在赤壁对垒。孙权的兵马大都督周瑜心胸狭隘,嫉妒诸葛亮的才干,准备借机置诸葛亮于死地,限他十天造十万支箭,否则军法严惩。诸葛亮成竹在胸,利用曹操多疑的性格和大雾的自然条件,安排了一出草船借箭的好戏。

Cao Cao led a massive army of one million soldiers on a southern campaign. Sun Quan, who, recognizing his own weakness, formed an alliance with Liu Bei to resist Cao Cao's forces, leading to a confrontation at Chibi. Zhou Yu, the Commander-in-Chief of Sun Quan's army, was narrow-minded and jealous of Zhuge Liang's exceptional talent. He saw an opportunity to put Zhuge Liang in a difficult position and issued a strict ultimatum: Zhuge Liang must produce 100,000 arrows within ten days, or face severe military punishment. Zhuge Liang remained confident and had a clever plan up his sleeve. He took advantage of Cao Cao's suspicious personality and foggy natural conditions to arrange a good play of borrowing arrows with thatched boats.

二、戏剧舞台 Theatre Stages

第一幕

Act 1

——

周瑜设计害孔明　孔明愿立军令状

Zhou Yu's Plot to Harm Zhuge Liang; Zhuge Liang Takes

Military Oath to Accomplish the Impossible

【人物】　周瑜、诸葛亮、鲁肃、军士

【Characters】　Zhou Yu, Zhuge Liang, Lu Su, Soldiers

【场景】　周瑜军帐

【Scene】　Zhou Yu's tent

【剧本】

【Script】

旁白：曹操大军挥师南下,孙权和刘备结成同盟,双方在赤壁对垒。周瑜嫉妒诸葛亮的才干,担心以后他成为东吴的威胁,定下计谋准备加害于他。这一天,周瑜请诸葛亮商议军事。

Narrator: Cao Cao leads his large army southward. Sun Quan and Liu Bei form an alliance to confront Cao Cao at Chibi. Zhou Yu, jealous of Zhuge Liang's talent and fearing him as a future threat to East Wu, decides to devise a plan to harm him. One day, Zhou Yu invites Zhuge Liang to discuss military affairs.

周瑜：(认真)我们马上就要跟曹军交战了。请问先生,在大

161

江上交战,用什么兵器最好?

Zhou Yu: (Seriously) We are about to engage in a battle with Cao Cao's forces. I would like to ask you a question, sir. What weapon is best suited for fighting on the river?

诸葛亮:(毫不犹豫)当然是用弓箭最好。

Zhuge Liang: (Without hesitation) Undoubtedly, bows and arrows are the best choice.

周瑜:(点头)先生所言极是。(皱眉)可是现在军中缺箭,能否请先生负责监造十万支箭?(故作严肃地说)这是大事,还请先生不要推脱。

Zhou Yu: (Nods) Your words are wise. (Frowning) However, we are facing a shortage of arrows. Can I request that you oversee the production of one hundred thousand arrows? (Pretending to be serious) This is a crucial matter, and I hope you won't refuse.

诸葛亮:(拱手)既然都督吩咐,自然愿意效劳。只是不知道这十万支箭什么时候要?

Zhuge Liang: (Making a bow with hands folded in front) Since Your Commander has given the order, I am surely willing to serve. I only wonder when you will need these one hundred thousand arrows?

周瑜:(试探)十天能造好吗?

Zhou Yu: (Tentatively) Can you complete the task in ten days?

诸葛亮:(关心)眼下大战在即,十天的话,恐怕会误了大事。

Zhuge Liang: (Worried) With the imminent battle approaching, I'm afraid ten days would hinder our cause.

周瑜:(惊诧)那几天能够造好?

Zhou Yu: (Surprised) Then how many days do you need?

诸葛亮:(自信)只要三天。

Zhuge Liang: (Confidently) Only three days.

周瑜:(紧逼)军中无戏言。此话当真?

Zhou Yu:（Pressing hard）There is no jesting in war. Are you serious?

诸葛亮:(斩钉截铁)我愿意立下军令状,三天造不好的话,甘受惩罚。(书写军令状)不过,今天来不及了,从明天算起吧。三天后,请到江边取箭。

Zhuge Liang:（Decisively）I am willing to make a death warrant. If I fail to complete the task in three days, I will accept the punishment.（Writing down the warrant）However, it's too late to start today. Let's begin tomorrow, and in three days, you can collect the arrows by the river.

周瑜:(开心)先生赶快回去准备吧。(诸葛亮回去)

Zhou Yu:（Delighted）Sir, please go home and make the necessary preparations.（Zhuge Liang takes his leave）

鲁肃:(困惑)三天怎能造得了十万支箭呢?

Lu Su:（Puzzled）How is it possible to make one hundred thousand arrows in three days?

周瑜:(冷笑)这是他自寻死路,又不是我逼他的。军令状在此,到时他只有死路一条。(吩咐军士)告诉工匠,尽量拖延,这样肯定会误了工期的。哈哈,到时看我怎么治他。

Zhou Yu:（Sneering）He has brought this upon himself; I did not force him. The death warrant is here, and when the time comes, he will have no escape.（To the soldiers）Inform the craftsmen to deliberately delay their work, ensuring that they miss the deadline. Haha, let's see how I punish him then.

第二幕

Act 2

———

孔明自有锦囊妙计　鲁肃答应掩人耳目

Zhuge Liang Devises an Ingenious Plan; Lu Su Agrees to Conceal the Truth

【人物】 诸葛亮、鲁肃

【Characters】 Zhuge Liang, Lu Su

【场景】 诸葛亮军帐

【Scene】 In Zhuge Liang's tent

【剧本】

【Script】

旁白：鲁肃心中不解，向诸葛亮打探消息。

Narrator：Lu Su, feeling conflicted, is seeking information from Zhuge Liang.

诸葛亮：在三天之内怎么能造十万支箭呢？你一定要帮助我。

Zhuge Liang: How can I possibly make one hundred thousand arrows in three days? I need your help.

鲁肃：(冷笑)这是你自找的麻烦，我怎么帮得了你？

Lu Su:（Sneering）You brought the trouble on yourself. How can I possibly help you?

诸葛亮：请你借给我二十条船，每条船上要三十名军士，用青布幔子遮起来，在船的两边扎上一千多个草靶子。

Zhuge Liang: I am looking to you for a loan of twenty boats, each manned with thirty soldiers. I want blue cotton screens and bundles of straw targets lashed to the sides of the boats.

鲁肃：这个没有问题。(困惑)但这与造箭有什么关系呢？

Lu Su: That's not a problem.（Puzzled）But what does this have to do with making arrows?

诸葛亮：(微笑)这你就不用管了，我自有妙用，保证在第三天有十万支箭就是了。(严肃地说)请你一定要保密，不能让都督知道，否则我的计划就泡汤了。

Zhuge Liang:（Smiling）You don't need to worry about that. I have good use for them. It is guaranteed that those fixed number of arrows will be delivered on time.（Speaking seriously）But on no account must you let the commander know, or my scheme will be wrecked.

鲁肃:（爽快）好的,我答应你。

Lu Su:（Unhesitatingly）Alright, I promise you.

第三幕

Act 3

———

孔明草船借箭　周瑜甘拜下风

Zhuge Liang's Ruse Triumphs; Zhou Yu Admits Defeat

【人物】　诸葛亮、周瑜、曹操、鲁肃、军士

【**Characters**】　Zhuge Liang, Zhou Yu, Cao Cao, Lu Su, Soldiers

【场景】　船上

【**Scene**】　On a boat

【剧本】

【**Script**】

旁白:鲁肃按照诸葛亮的要求准备停当,但两天都过去了,仍不见诸葛亮有什么动作,鲁肃心中十分着急。直到第三天的四更时分,大雾漫天,诸葛亮秘密地把鲁肃请到船上。

Narrator: Lu Su has prepared everything as per Zhuge Liang's instructions. However, two days have passed, and there is no sign of Zhuge Liang making arrows. Lu Su is becoming increasingly anxious. At midnight on the third day, a thick fog covers the surroundings. Zhuge Liang secretly invites Lu Su onto a boat.

鲁肃:(疑惑)这么晚了,找我来有什么事情吗?

Lu Su: (Perplexed) Why have you called me at this late hour?

诸葛亮:(愉快)请你和我一起取箭去。

Zhuge Liang: (Joyfully) Join me in retrieving the arrows.

鲁肃:(吃惊)到哪里去取?

Lu Su: (Surprised) Retrieve them from where?

诸葛亮:不用多问,去了你就知道了。(吩咐军士)把二十条船用绳索连接起来,朝北岸进发。逼近曹军的营寨后,把船头朝西,船尾朝东,一字摆开,然后一边擂鼓,一边大声呐喊。

Zhuge Liang: Do not ask, you will see. (Ordering the soldiers) Fasten the twenty boats by long ropes and move over to the north bank. When we approach Cao's camp, align the boats in a single line, with the front facing west and the rear facing east. Drum and shout loudly.

鲁肃:(吃惊)如果曹军出兵迎战,我们如何是好?

Lu Su: (Startled) But what should we do if they attack us?

诸葛亮:(微笑)这么大的雾,曹操一定不敢派兵出来。我们只管饮酒取乐,天亮了就回去。

Zhuge Liang:(Smiling) I doubt that Cao Cao's fleet will be sent out in this foggy day. Go on with drinking. We will go back when dawn breaks.

旁白:曹操听到鼓声和呐喊声,心中疑惑,派兵怕有闪失,就下令调集一万名弓箭手朝他们射箭,不让靠近。一时箭如雨发,飞向诸葛亮的草船。

Narrator: Cao Cao hears the drums and shouts. He becomes suspicious, fearing a trap. He orders ten thousand archers to shoot at the suspicious targets, preventing their approach. Arrows rain down, heading towards Zhuge Liang's thatched boats.

军士：报，曹军的箭把船的一边扎得密密麻麻，船都有些倾斜了。

Soldiers: Report! Cao's arrows have densely struck one side of the boats, causing them to tilt.

诸葛亮：掉转船头，把船头朝东，船尾朝西，继续擂鼓呐喊。

Zhuge Liang: Turn the boats around, with the front facing east and the rear facing west. Keep drumming and shouting.

军士：遵命。

Soldiers: Understood.

旁白：天渐渐亮了，但大雾还没有散。这时候，船两边的草靶子上都插满了箭。

Narrator：The day gradually grows brighter, but the thick fog has not lifted. The straw targets on both sides of the boats are now filled with arrows.

诸葛亮：现在应当已经有十万支箭了，我们回去吧。大家谢谢曹丞相。

Zhuge Liang: We must have already got enough arrows. Let's say thanks to Prime Minister Cao before we go back.

军士：谢谢曹丞相的箭。

Soldiers: Prime Minister, we thank you for the arrows.

鲁肃：（佩服）先生真是神人也。我马上向都督禀报，任务完成了。

Lu Su:（Admiring）Sir, you truly possess divine insight. I will promptly inform the commander that the mission has been accomplished.

周瑜：（听到禀报后，长叹）诸葛亮神机妙算，我真是比他差远了。

Zhou Yu:（Upon hearing the report, sighs deeply）Zhuge Liang's

167

brilliant strategies are truly awe-inspiring. I am no match for him.

三、故事赏析 Story Analysis

孙权和刘备联合抗击曹操，大敌当前，周瑜却嫉妒诸葛亮的才能，欲置诸葛亮于死地，故意提出让诸葛亮十天造十万支箭。诸葛亮识破周瑜的奸计，面对不可能完成的任务，却成竹在胸地表示只需要三天。在鲁肃的帮助下，诸葛亮利用大雾的天气条件和曹操多疑的性格特征，利用草船从曹操那里成功"借"了十万支箭，立下奇功。这个故事情节跌宕起伏，引人入胜，也成功刻画了诸葛亮的多智、周瑜的妒才、鲁肃的忠厚和曹操的多疑等不同的人物形象。

In the face of the formidable enemy Cao Cao, Sun Quan and Liu Bei joined forces. However, Zhou Yu, consumed by jealousy of Zhuge Liang's talent, plotted to trap him by assigning him the impossible task of producing 100,000 arrows in ten days. Seeing through Zhou Yu's scheme, Zhuge Liang confidently claimed that he only needed three days. With the assistance of Lu Su, Zhuge Liang capitalized on the foggy weather and Cao Cao's inherent suspicion to successfully "borrow" 100,000 arrows from Cao Cao, achieving a remarkable feat. This story exhibits a captivating narrative with its dramatic twists and turns. It effectively portrays various characters, showcasing Zhuge Liang's strategic genius, Zhou Yu's envy, Lu Su's loyalty, and Cao Cao's suspicious nature.

第三节

Section Three

对酒当歌

The Ballad of the Short-Song

一、故事梗概 Synopsis

建安十三年冬，曹操率领大军南下，打算消灭孙权和刘备，统一天下，双方在赤壁对垒。十一月十五日，天气晴朗，风平浪静，当夜曹操大摆宴席宴请文武百官。曹操认为破敌之日可待，心情大好，酒酣之余，慷慨而唱《短歌行》，表达了自己的雄心壮志和对贤才的渴慕。

In the winter of the thirteenth year of the Jian'an era, Cao Cao led a massive army on a southward campaign to eliminate Sun Quan and Liu Bei, with the aim of unifying the realm. The two opposing forces confronted each other at Chibi. On a clear and serene day, November 15th, Cao Cao hosted a grand feast, inviting his civil and military officials. Buoyed by his confidence in the imminent victory, Cao Cao sang "The Ballad of the Short-Song" after enjoying the wine, expressing his ambitious aspirations and admiration for talented individuals.

二、戏剧舞台 Theatre Stages

第一幕

Act 1

————

徐庶用计远离战祸

Xu Shu's Cunning Plan to Avoid the Battle

【人物】 曹操、徐庶、臧霸、军士

【Characters】 Cao Cao, Xu Shu, Zang Ba, Soldiers

【场景】 曹操营帐

【Scene】 Cao Cao's camp

【剧本】

【Script】

旁白：曹操采纳了庞统的建议，将战船连接在一起以解决北方士兵不习惯江上作战的问题，却埋下了容易被火攻的隐患。徐庶识破了这个计策的用意，找到了一条自救的出路，安排人员散布"西凉兵将要进攻许昌"的谣言。

Narrator: Cao Cao accepts Pang Tong's suggestion to connect the warships together. This addresses the issue of his northern soldiers' unfamiliarity with river warfare, but unknowingly creates a vulnerability to fire attacks. Xu Shu, who astutely understands the purpose behind this strategy, seeks a way to save himself by spreading rumors that Xiliang troops are planning to attack Xuchang.

军士:(急报)报丞相,营寨有传言,西凉的马腾、韩遂有意谋反,带兵奔许昌而来。

Soldiers: (Reports urgently) Prime Minister, a rumor is running around the camps that Ma Teng and Han Sui intend to rebel and march from Xiliang to attack the capital.

曹操:(吃惊)我这次领兵南征,担忧的就是西凉的马腾等人。(沉吟)虽然传言不一定属实,但也不得不防。各位有什么妙计吗?

Cao Cao: (Surprised) The only anxiety I have felt in this expedition was about the possible doings of Ma Teng and Han Sui. (Contemplating) Although I am uncertain of the rumor's accuracy, it is crucial to stay alert. What ideas have you got?

徐庶:(上前行礼)承蒙丞相器重,但我至今未有寸功。我愿带领一支兵马,前往散关驻扎把守。如有紧要之事,再行报告。

Xu Shu: (Steps forward and bows) I am grateful for the Prime Minister's trust, but I have really done nothing in return. I am willing to lead a force and immediately march to the San Pass and guard this entrance. If there is any urgent matter, I will report it at once.

曹操:(高兴)如果你能前去,我就高枕无忧了。散关的驻军由你统领,另拨给你三千马步军,再任臧霸为先锋助你一臂之力。须星夜前去,不得延误。

Cao Cao: (Delighted) If you would do this, I should be quite at my ease. There are already troops at the Pass, who will be under your command, and now I will assign you three thousand of horses and infantrymen, and Zang Ba shall lead in the van and march quickly.

臧霸:(高声)听从丞相调遣。

Zang Ba: (Loudly) I will obey the Prime Minister's orders.

徐庶:(欣喜)谢丞相,兵贵神速,今晚我们就出发。

Xu Shu: (Joyful) Thank you, Prime Minister. In warfare, swiftness

is of the essence. We will set out tonight.

第二幕

Act 2

——

宴长江曹操横槊赋诗

Banquet on the Changjiang River—Cao Cao's Poetic Inspiration

【人物】 曹操、荀攸、刘馥、文武官员、众将士

【Characters】 Cao Cao, Xun You, Liu Fu, Civil and Military Officials, Generals and Soldiers

【场景】 曹操营帐

【Scene】 Cao Cao's camp

【剧本】

【Script】

旁白：徐庶带兵走后，曹操不再担忧后方许都的防卫问题，巡视一番，看到兵强马壮，士气高昂，心中非常高兴，准备宴请群臣。

Narrator: After Xu Shu leads his troops away, Cao Cao's concerns about the defense of the capital are dispelled. As he inspects his strong and confident army, his heart overflows with joy. He decides to host a grand banquet and invite all his officials.

曹操：(高兴) 今日在大船上摆设酒宴，请各位欣赏歌舞，尽情畅饮。

Cao Cao: (Joyfully) Today, I have prepared a splendid banquet on the ship. I invite all of you to enjoy the music, dancing, and indulge in unlimited drinks.

众将士：(叩拜) 谢丞相。

Generals and Soldiers: (Kowtow) Well, thank you, Prime Minister.

曹操：(歌舞罢，起身把盏)自我举兵以来，东征西伐，为国家讨伐逆贼，灭掉了袁绍、袁术、吕布等人，目前就剩下江南尚未收复。现如今我有百万雄师，更有各位在帐前效力，何愁东吴不灭，大功告成指日可待了。等到收复江南，天下太平之时，各位与我共享富贵，以乐太平。

Cao Cao: (After singing and dancing, he rises and raises his cup) Since I first dispatched troops, I have fought in the east and the west. With the aim of removing evil from the state, I have eliminated Yuan Shao, Yuan Shu, and Lü Bu, etc. Now, the only region needed to be recaptured is the southern region. With a hundred legions under my command, I depend on you, gentlemen, and have no doubt of my final success. Once I have conquered the South Land, there will be no trouble in overall victory. Then, we shall enjoy wealth and honor, and revel in peace.

文武官员：(起身拜谢)愿早奏凯歌！承蒙丞相恩德。

Civil and Military Officials: (They all rise and bow to express their appreciation) We trust that we may soon report complete victory, and we shall all repose in the shade of your good fortune and benevolence.

众将士：(高举火把欢呼)早奏凯歌，早奏凯歌，早奏凯歌……（欢呼声响彻云霄）

Generals and Soldiers: (Raising their torches and cheering) Victory, victory, victory ... (Cheers resound through the sky)

曹操：(大声地)好！共饮此酒！

Cao Cao: (Loudly) Excellent! Let us drink together!

文武官员：(齐呼)谢丞相！（饮酒毕）

Civil and Military Officials: (Shouting in unison) Thank you, Prime Minister! (They finish drinking)

曹操:(饮至半夜,酒酣,遥指南岸)我笑周瑜、鲁肃不识天时,竟敢以卵击石。如今已有投降之人作为内应,真是天助我也。(随即仰天大笑)

Cao Cao: (Drinking till midnight, inebriated, pointing to the south bank) How ridiculous it is that Zhou Yu and Lu Su are unaware of the opportune moment and dare to strike a stone with an egg! Heaven is aiding me by bringing upon them the misfortune of the desertion of their most trusted friends. (Immediately bursts into laughter, gazing up at the sky)

荀攸:(拜首上前)丞相慎言,恐有泄漏啊。

Xun You: (Bowing and stepping forward) Prime Minister, say nothing of these things lest they become known to the enemy.

曹操:(大笑)在座各位,都是我的心腹,言之又有何妨!(众人皆笑)

Cao Cao: (Laughing) You are all my trusty subordinates, both officers and humble attendants. Why should I refrain? (Everyone laughs)

曹操:(遥指夏口)我更笑刘备、诸葛亮,以蝼蚁之力撼泰山,何其愚也! 哈哈哈哈!

Cao Cao: (Pointing to Xiakou) You and your feeble force, Liu Bei and Zhuge Liang, are not even worth considering. How foolish of you to attempt to shake the mighty Mount Tai! Hahaha!

文武官员:(齐声高呼)孙刘联盟,不足挂齿!

Civil and Military Officials: (Shouting in unison) The alliance of Sun Quan and Liu Bei is not worth a mention!

曹操:(环顾四周自语)今年我五十有四了,如得江南,还有个愿望。江南有二乔女子,都是国色天香,我在漳水之上修建铜雀

台，若能和二乔一起欢度晚年，平生都如愿了。（言罢大笑）

Cao Cao: (Looking around and soliloquizing) Now that I am fifty-four, if I acquire the South Land, I will have the means to rejoice. There are two incomparably beautiful women, Elder Qiao and Younger Qiao (referring to the wives of Sun Quan and Zhou Yu). With my palace built on the Zhang River, conquering the South Land will allow me to place these two fair ladies in the Bronze Bird Tower, where they will bring joy in my later years. My desires will then be completely attained. (Then laughing)

文武官员：（齐声）恭贺丞相。

Civil and Military Officials: (Chorus) Congratulations, Prime Minister.

曹操：（大喝）取槊来！（又转身向近侍）取酒来！

Cao Cao: (Shouting loudly) Bring me the spear! (Then turns to the bodyguard) Fetch the wine!

曹操：（洒酒祭天地，横槊而叹）我持此槊，破黄巾、擒吕布、灭袁术、败袁绍，深入塞北，直抵辽东，纵横天下，所向披靡，也不负大丈夫之志也。

Cao Cao: (Scattering wine as an offering to Heaven and Earth, holding the spear and sighing) This is the spear that broke up the Yellow Scarves Rebellion, captured Lü Bu, destroyed Yuan Shu, and subdued Yuan Shao, whose armies are now mine. In the north, my kingdom reached Liaodong, and stretched out over the whole south. I have never failed in my ambition.

曹操：（再叹）此时此刻，上有皓月当空，下有江波荡漾，此情此景，感慨系之。我当作歌，汝等和之。

Cao Cao: (Sighing once more) At this very moment, there is a bright moon in the sky and rippling waves in the river. The present scene moves me to the depths, and I will sing a song in which you shall accompany me.

文武官员、众将士:（叩拜）好。

Civil and Military Officials, Generals and Soldiers: (Kowtowing) Very well.

曹操:（鼓乐钟鸣,慷慨陈词,饱含热泪,把盏对歌）

Cao Cao: (Amidst the resounding drums and bells, delivering impassioned speeches with tears in his eyes, he raises his cup and begins to sing)

> 对酒当歌,人生几何！譬如朝露,去日苦多。
> 慨当以慷,忧思难忘。何以解忧？唯有杜康。
> 青青子衿,悠悠我心。但为君故,沉吟至今。
> 呦呦鹿鸣,食野之苹。我有嘉宾,鼓瑟吹笙。
> 明明如月,何时可掇？忧从中来,不可断绝。
> 越陌度阡,枉用相存。契阔谈讌,心念旧恩。
> 月明星稀,乌鹊南飞。绕树三匝,何枝可依？
> 山不厌高,海不厌深。周公吐哺,天下归心。

> Before wine, sing a song;
>
> How long is life, how long?
>
> It seems like morning dew
>
> With bygones gone with woe.
>
> O sing loud and sing free,
>
> And yet my cause frets me.
>
> What can kill sorrow mine?
>
> Nothing but Dukang Wine.
>
> Blue, blue the scholar gown
>
> Seek, seek I up and down.
>
> In your esteem I bow
>
> And have chanted till now.

The deer each to each bleat;

Afield they wormwood eat.

I have good guests today;

The lute and flute we play.

Fair, fair the moon does shine;

Could I have it? I pine!

My heart's laden with care,

Which seems to stay for e'er.

Through the field lies the lane;

It's for you, not in vain.

We talk throughout repast;

Rememb'ring your grace past.

The moon's bright and stars few;

Fly south magpie and crow.

Thrice they go round the birch,

But on which bough to perch?

Let mounts be high and steep

And the seas broad and deep.

O our sage Prince of Chough,

To your side all would go.

（赵彦春[1]翻译）

旁白：众人和音，欢笑一堂。

Narrator： The crowd sing along with him, and they are all exceedingly merry.

曹操：（笑罢）刘馥何在？

---

1 赵彦春. 翻译诗学散论[M]. 青岛：青岛出版社，2007.

Cao Cao: (Laughing) Where is Liu Fu?

刘馥：(上前拜首)臣在。

Liu Fu: (Steps forward and bows respectfully) Yes.

曹操：依你看来，我的这首《短歌行》写得如何呀？

Cao Cao: What do you think of my song?

刘馥：(思忖片刻)丞相的歌，词意深邃，合于音韵，文采洋溢，精妙非常。(停顿)但是……

Liu Fu: (Pondering for a moment) Prime Minister, your lyrics are profound in meaning, perfectly aligned with the rhyme, brimming with literary elegance, and exceptionally exquisite. (Pauses) However ...

曹操：但讲无妨。

Cao Cao: Feel free to speak up.

刘馥：(拱手而答)丞相果真要我直言不讳？

Liu Fu: (Making a bow with hands folded in front) Does the Prime Minister truly want me to speak my mind?

曹操：(转身一挥衣袍)那自然。

Cao Cao: (Turns around and waves his robe) Certainly.

刘馥：(犹豫)丞相的歌词虽然文采盖世，只是似乎有不祥之言。

Liu Fu: (Hesitating) Although the lyrics of the Prime Minister's song are remarkably eloquent, they seem to contain some ominous words.

曹操：有何不祥？

Cao Cao: What ill-omened words did I use?

刘馥："月明星稀,乌鹊南飞。绕树三匝,何枝可依？"这几句不大吉利。眼下南征在即,大军临战之时,这几句不祥之言,有损军威。

Liu Fu: "The moon's bright and stars few; Fly south magpie and crow. Thrice they go round the birch, But on which bough to perch?" are ill-omened. As we are on the verge of a southern expedition, with the army about to engage in battle, such ominous words will undermine the military's morale.

曹操:（大怒）你怎敢败我诗兴！（手起一槊,刺死刘馥。众人都惊吓不已,曹操回过神来也惊叫倒地。）

Cao Cao:（Enraged）How dare you try to dampen my spirits? （He raises his spear and fatally stabs Liu Fu. Everyone is shocked. Later Cao Cao regains his senses and falls to the ground。）

文武官员:（赶紧扶起曹操）丞相,丞相,丞相……（遂罢宴）

Civil and Military Officials:（Hastily helping Cao Cao get up） Prime Minister, Prime Minister, Prime Minister ...（The banquet abruptly ended）

三、故事赏析 Story Analysis

赤壁大战之前,曹操踌躇满志,准备一举荡平孙权和刘备,统一天下。在宴请群臣时,曹操和众人开怀畅饮,畅谈人生,一边饮酒,一边高歌。曹操横槊而作的《短歌行》表达了自己的雄心壮志,也表达了对人才的渴求之情。故事情节慷慨激昂,跌宕起伏。最后曹操酒醉误杀了直言的刘馥,宴会草草收场,也预示着赤壁大战曹军的失败。

Before the Battle of Chibi, Cao Cao was filled with ambitious aspirations. He was preparing to conquer Sun Quan and Liu Bei in one fell swoop, thus achieving the unification of the land. During a banquet with his officials, Cao Cao and the others indulged in lively drinking and engaged in discussions about life. Cao Cao composed "The Ballad of the Short-Song", which expressed his grand ambitions and his longing for talented individuals. The story unfolds with passionate and tumultuous plots. Ultimately, in a drunken state, Cao Cao mistakenly killed the outspoken Liu Fu, abruptly concluding the banquet and foreshadowing his failure in the Battle of Chibi.

七擒七纵

Zhuge Liang's Seven Victories Over Meng Huo

一、故事梗概 Synopsis

蜀汉后主建兴三年,蜀国西南三郡叛乱,当地的人民都很信服部落首领孟获,因此孟获是平叛的主要目标人物。针对南中地理偏远等实际情况,诸葛亮制订了"攻心为上,攻城为下;心战为上,兵战为下"的策略。在迅速平定了三郡的反叛之后,诸葛亮将孟获捉住了七次,又放了七次,最后孟获心服口服,不再反叛。

During the third year of the Latter Ruler Liu Shan's reign (AD 225), three counties in the southwest of Shu rebelled. The local people had great faith in the tribal leader Meng Huo, who was the primary target of suppression. Given the remote geographical location of the southeastern regions, Zhuge Liang devised a strategy focused on winning the hearts and minds of people. He emphasized the importance of prioritizing sentiment of the people over the capture of cities, believing that this approach would yield superior results compared to direct military confrontation. After swiftly suppressing the rebellion in the three counties, Zhuge Liang captured Meng Huo on seven occasions, only to release him each time. Eventually, Meng Huo accepted defeat completely, bringing an end to his rebellious actions.

二、戏剧舞台 Theatre Stages

第一幕

Act 1

————

诸葛亮计定南中

Zhuge Liang's Strategy to Subdue the Meng Tribes in Southeast

【人物】 诸葛亮、马谡、魏延

【**Characters**】 Zhuge Liang, Ma Su, Wei Yan

【场景】 诸葛亮营帐

【**Scene**】 Zhuge Liang's camp

【剧本】

【**Script**】

旁白：蜀汉西南三郡经常反叛，诸葛亮率军征讨，和将领们商议彻底平叛的策略。

Narrator: The three southwestern commanderies of Shu Han frequently rebel. Zhuge Liang leads troops to suppress these rebellions and discusses with his generals strategies for completely pacifying the region.

诸葛亮：南中三郡反叛，以孟获为首。各位有什么良策？

Zhuge Liang: The rebellion of the Meng tribes in the southeastern region, led by Meng Huo, poses a threat. Do any of you have a viable plan to quell this uprising?

魏延：我愿为先锋，杀他个片甲不留。

Wei Yan: I suggest myself fight in the van and exterminating them, leaving no survivors.

诸葛亮：打败他们很容易，但怎么能够长久呢？

Zhuge Liang: While defeating them may be achievable, how can we prevent future rebellions and achieve long-term stability?

马谡：（建言）南蛮之地，路途遥远，山高路险，就算今天把他们打败了，等我们退兵之后，他们还会再起反叛之心。兵法有云：攻心为上，攻城为下；心战为上，兵战为下。望丞相明察。

Ma Su: (Offering advice) The southeastern territory is remote and challenging, making it difficult to maintain control. Even if we defeat them today, they will harbor rebellious sentiments once our forces withdraw. As one military tactic teaches, it is best to attack hearts before attacking cities. Winning over their sentiment is more crucial than engaging in direct combat. I hope the Prime Minister can discern the wisdom in this approach.

诸葛亮：（赞许）心战为上，正合我意。一定要彻底收服他们，以后就不会再兴师动众了。

Zhuge Liang: (Approvingly) You read my inmost thoghts. We must completely subdue them, so we won't have to mobilize our forces again in the future.

第二幕

Act 2

———

诸葛亮一擒孟获

Zhuge Liang's First Capture of Meng Huo

【人物】 诸葛亮、孟获、蜀兵

【**Characters**】 Zhuge Liang, Meng Huo, Shu Soldiers

【场景】 中军大帐

【**Scene**】 Zhuge Liang's camp

【剧本】

【**Script**】

旁白：诸葛亮安排王平、关索二人率兵与孟获交战，假装败退，将孟获引到峡谷，大将魏延在那已等候多时，将孟获生擒活捉，押到了中军大帐。孟获第一次被擒。

Narrator：Zhuge Liang instructs Wang Ping and Guan Suo to lead their troops in a battle against Meng Huo. They feign defeat and lure Meng Huo into a narrow valley, where General Wei Yan has been laying in wait. Wei Yan successfully captures Meng Huo alive and brings him back to Zhuge Liang's camp. This marks the first time Meng Huo has been captured.

蜀兵：（快步跑来，站定后双手抱拳，大声道）报丞相，我军大胜，活捉孟获！

Shu Soldiers: (Hurrying over and standing at attention, with clasped fists) Reporting to the Prime Minister, our army achieved a great victory and captured Meng Huo alive!

诸葛亮：（高兴）好，带上来！（孟获双手被反绑着押了进来）

Zhuge Liang: (Joyful) Excellent, bring him here! (Meng Huo is brought forward with his hands tied behind his back)

诸葛亮：（笑问）孟获，此次被擒，你是否服气？

Zhuge Liang: (Smilingly asks) Meng Huo, you are my prisoner. Will you submit?

孟获：（很不服气的样子）是我不小心中了你的计，才在峡谷之中被捉拿，怎能叫人心服？

Meng Huo: (Showing strong reluctance) Why should I submit? You happened to find me in a narrow place; that is all.

诸葛亮:(走上前去,帮孟获解开绳子,和蔼地说)既然不服, 我就放你回去。咱们择日再战,怎么样?

Zhuge Liang: (Approaching Meng Huo, untying the ropes, and speaking kindly) Since you still refuse to submit, I will release you for now. Let us choose another day to continue our battle. How does that sound?

孟获:你放我回去重整军马,我们再战。如果再被你捉住,我 就服输!(说完灰溜溜地跑了)

Meng Huo: If you release me I shall return; and when I have set my army in order, I shall come to fight you again. However, if you catch me once more, I will submit. (Saying this, he slips away dejectedly)

第三幕

Act 3

———

诸葛亮二擒孟获

Zhuge Liang's Second Capture of Meng Huo

【人物】 诸葛亮、孟获、众将领

【Characters】 Zhuge Liang, Meng Huo, Generals

【场景】 诸葛亮营帐

【Scene】 Zhuge Liang's camp

【剧本】

【Script】

旁白:孟获逃回山寨,依赖地势险要,固守不出。孟获部下因吃了败仗,受到惩罚,趁孟获酒醉将他绑了,送到诸葛亮营寨。

Narrator：Meng Huo flees back to his camp in the mountains, relying on the treacherous terrain to fortify his position and refusing to venture out. After Meng Huo's men are defeated and punished, they take advantage of Meng Huo's drunken state to tie him up and deliver him to Zhuge Liang's camp.

诸葛亮：(依然笑着问道)你上次说如果再被捉住,就会心服。今天投降不投降?

Zhuge Liang:（Still smiling）You said once before that if you were captured again, you would give in. Now, will you yield?

孟获：(怒气冲冲)这次是手下出卖我,不是你有本事,我肯定不服!

Meng Huo:（Furious）This capture is not your work. It is the work of these minions of mine who betrayed me. I will not yield on this!

诸葛亮：那我这次仍旧把你放了,看你还能怎样。

Zhuge Liang: If I free you again, what then?

孟获：你放我回去,我带上兵,咱们一决胜负。如果再被捉住,我就实心实意地归顺,再也不反叛了。

Meng Huo: Release me, and I will gather my forces for a final battle. If I am captured again, I will genuinely surrender and never rebel again.

诸葛亮：如果再捉住你,还不服气,我就不会再饶恕你了(诸葛亮摆了摆手,放他走了)

Zhuge Liang: If you refuse to yield next time you are captured, I shall hardly pardon you.（Zhuge Liang waves his hand and lets him go.）

第四幕

Act 4

———

诸葛亮三擒孟获

Zhuge Liang's Third Capture of Meng Huo

【人物】 诸葛亮、孟获、孟优、众将领

【Characters】 Zhuge Liang, Meng Huo, Meng You, Generals

【场景】 诸葛亮营帐

【Scene】 Zhuge Liang's camp

【剧本】

【Script】

旁白：孟获回到山寨，闷闷不乐。其弟孟优献计说，自己假装进献财宝作为内应，然后孟获在半夜进攻，这样里应外合就可以打败诸葛亮。

Narrator：Meng Huo returns to his camp feeling gloomy. His younger brother, Meng You, comes up with a plan. Meng You will pretend to offer treasures as a ploy, luring Zhuge Liang into a trap. They will then launch a surprise attack at midnight. They believe that this combination of internal and external forces will be enough to defeat Zhuge Liang.

诸葛亮：(微微一笑)孟获，我已经等你多时了，你再回头看看谁被捉住了。

Zhuge Liang: (Smiling) Meng Huo, I have been waiting for you. Take a look and see who has been captured.

孟获：(回头，看到孟优已被捆绑，哀叹)弟弟……

Meng Huo: (Looking back, seeing Meng You tied up, lamenting) My brother ...

诸葛亮：你弟弟进献财宝,却带来了许多士兵。我就知道你们的伎俩。这点雕虫小技怎么能瞒过我呢？现在你还有什么话说？

Zhuge Liang: Your brother pretended to offer treasures, but he brought many soldiers instead. I knew your petty scheme. Did you really think I would not see through it? But here you are once more in my power. Now do you yield?

孟获：(垂头丧气)被你看破,中了你的计,我还是不服。

Meng Huo: (Depressed) I have been exposed, falling into your trap. No, I will not yield.

诸葛亮：(挥挥手)这次还放你回去,如果再捉住你了就绝不宽恕。

Zhuge Liang: (Waving his hands) Fine, I will let you go again. But if you are captured again, there will be no forgiveness.

第五幕

Act 5

———

诸葛亮七擒孟获

Zhuge Liang's Seventh Capture of Meng Huo

【人物】 诸葛亮、孟获、众将领

【Characters】 Zhuge Liang, Meng Huo, Generals

【场景】 诸葛亮营帐

【Scene】 Zhuge Liang's camp

【剧本】

【Script】

旁白：就这样捉了放,放了捉,捉了又放。第七次,孟获搬来救兵,指望藤甲兵能够打败诸葛亮。这些藤甲兵刀枪不入,不料遭到火攻,又被打败。孟获又被抓住,被押到诸葛亮营帐。

Narrator: And so the cycle continues, with Meng Huo being caught and then released, released and then caught. In their seventh battle, Meng Huo resorts to his rattan-armored troops, hoping they can defeat Zhuge Liang. However, the specially made rattans, which are excellent protection against swords and arrows, are also highly flammable. Zhuge Liang's fire attack quickly consumes the rattans, and Meng Huo is once again defeated. He is captured and taken to Zhuge Liang's camp.

诸葛亮:(微笑)孟获,这次是第七次被捉了。还和以前一样,仍旧放你回去,你可领兵再决胜负。

Zhuge Liang: (Smiling) Meng Huo, this is the seventh time you have been caught. Just like before, I will release you again. Gather your troops and let's settle the matter once and for all.

孟获:(惭愧万分,流泪)丞相,您对我是七擒七纵,仁至义尽,我彻底服输。我发誓:从今以后,再也不反叛了。

Meng Huo: (Deeply ashamed, shedding tears) Prime Minister, you have captured and released me seven times. Your mercy and righteousness have touched me deeply. I surrender completely. I swear from this day forward, I will never rebel again.

众将领:(同声)丞相威武! 恭喜丞相,平定南中。

Generals: (In unison) Prime Minister is mighty! Congratulations to the Prime Minister for pacifying the southern region.

诸葛亮:都是大家的功劳,明日起班师回朝。

Zhuge Liang: It's thanks to everyone's efforts. Tomorrow, we will return to the court.

三、故事赏析 Story Analysis

《三国演义》用了四个章回描写了七擒七纵的故事,形象地表现了诸葛亮的足智多谋,终使孟获心悦诚服,稳定了蜀汉政权。在平定叛乱的过程中,诸葛亮采用了攻心为上的策略,消除了蛮兵的反叛心理。这个故事也告诉我们,在处理事情时要灵活、正确地运用策略。

The Three Kingdoms Romance uses four chapters to recount the captivating tale of Meng Huo's seven-time capture and release. This vividly portrays Zhuge Liang's strategic brilliance and clever tactics, which ultimately led to Meng Huo's sincere surrender and contributed to the stability of the Shu Han regime. Throughout the pacification of the rebellion, Zhuge Liang skillfully employed the hearts and minds strategy, effectively quelling rebellious sentiments among the soldiers in the southern region. This story serves as a powerful reminder of the importance of utilizing flexible and effective strategies when handling various situations.

第五节

Section Five

———

七步成诗

Composing a Poem Within Seven Steps

一、故事梗概 Synopsis

东汉末年，王室衰微，曹操权倾朝野，贵为丞相，后晋封魏王。曹操的四个儿子中，曹丕和曹植是继承王位的有力争夺者。曹植本来最受喜爱，才气过人却浮夸放纵，逐渐不被重用。次子曹丕稳重谨慎，后来被确立为王位继承人。曹操因病死后，曹丕继承魏王王位。曹丕嫉妒曹植的才华，又怀疑他以后可能成为自己的隐患，决定借机诛杀曹植。曹丕命令曹植在七步之内吟诗一首，否则将杀死他。曹植在七步之内出口成诗，以"豆"和"萁"比喻兄弟之情，劝诫曹丕不要骨肉相残，最终逃过一劫。这就是流传至今的七步成诗的故事。

During the declining years of the Eastern Han Dynasty, Cao Cao rose to power and became the Prime Minister. He was later titled

King Wei. Among his four sons, Cao Pi and Cao Zhi were strong con-tenders for the throne. Cao Zhi was initially favored because of his remarkable talent, but he gradually fell out of favor and lost influence due to his flamboyant and indulgent lifestyle. Cao Pi, the second son, was steady and cautious, and he eventually became the designated heir. After Cao Cao died, Cao Pi succeeded him as King Wei. However, Cao Pi became envious of Cao Zhi's brilliance and suspected that he would become a future threat. Cao Pi seized an opportunity to execute Cao Zhi and issued a command. Cao Zhi was to compose a poem within seven steps, or he would be killed. Within the limited time, Cao Zhi ingeniously crafted a poem using beans and a beanstalk as metaphors for brotherly love, urging against fratricidal acts. This dis-play of poetic prowess saved him from imminent death. The story of "Composing a Poem Within Seven Steps" has endured through gen-erations.

二、戏剧舞台 Theatre Stages

第一幕
Act 1

———

华歆进言曹丕杀害曹植
Hua Xin Suggests Cao Pi to Execute Cao Zhi

【人物】 曹丕、华歆、许诸

【Characters】 Cao Pi, Hua Xin, Xu Zhu

【场景】 王官内

【Scene】 Inside the Palace

【剧本】

【Script】

旁白：曹操因病不治而亡，由曹丕继承魏王之位。临淄侯曹植和萧怀侯曹熊是曹丕一母同胞的兄弟，没有前去为父亲吊丧。曹丕派人向两人问罪，曹熊畏罪自杀，曹植仍怠慢无礼。大臣华歆洞悉曹丕的心思，建议对曹植治罪。

Narrator: In the wake of Cao Cao's passing, Cao Pi assumes the throne as the new King of Wei. However, his brothers from the same mother, Cao Zhi, the Lord of Linzi, and Cao Xiong, the Lord of Xiaohuai, are noticeably absent from their father's funeral. Concerned about their absence, Cao Pi dispatches messengers to inquire about the reasons behind it. Cao Xiong, fearing punishment, chooses to take his own life. On the other hand, Cao Zhi displays negligence and disrespect towards his brother's authority. Sensing Cao Pi's intentions, Prime Minister Hua Xin suggests taking punitive action against Cao Zhi.

华歆：(察言观色)禀报魏王，先王宾天大礼时，临淄侯曹植居然不来奔丧，今日魏王继承王位又不来叩拜，实在是大逆不道。

Hua Xin: (Observing carefully) I have a report for Your Majesty. The Lord of Linzi Cao Zhi did not attend the grand funeral of the late King. Now that Your Majesty has ascended to the throne, Cao Zhi still refuses to pay his respects. This is an act of great treachery.

曹丕：(生气)是啊，三弟这不仅仅是对父王的不孝，也是对我的不恭敬，我岂能容忍。

Cao Pi: (Angrily) Indeed, my younger brother is disrespectful to our late father and shows no reverence towards me. I cannot tolerate this any longer.

华歆：(火上浇油)我听说临淄侯自诩才高八斗，还口出狂言，认为应当由他自己继承大位。

Hua Xin: (Provoking further) I've heard that the Lord of Linzi boasts of his exceptional talent and arrogantly believes he should be the rightful heir to the throne.

曹丕:（大怒）父王在世时把他宠坏了，他才恃才欺人。今天我必须治他的罪。许诸何在？

Cao Pi: (Enraged) He was indulged by our late father, relying on his talent to deceive others. Today, I must hold him accountable. Where is Xu Zhu?

许诸:（大声）末将在。

Xu Zhu: (Loudly) I'm here.

曹丕:（威严）命你立即前去捉拿曹植，带回来问罪。

Cao Pi: (Authoritatively) I command you to immediately go and apprehend Cao Zhi, bring him back for questioning.

许诸:（拱手）遵命。

Xu Zhu: (Making a bow with hands folded in front) Your command will be obeyed.

第二幕

Act 2

———

卞太后哭诉曹丕兄弟之情

Empress Bian Appeals to Cao Pi, Urging him to Value Brotherhood

【人物】 曹丕、卞太后

【Characters】 Cao Pi, Empress Bian

【场景】 王宫内

【Scene】 Inside the Palace

【剧本】

【Script】

旁白:曹丕之母卞太后,听到四子曹熊畏罪自杀的消息十分悲伤,又听到曹丕派人捉拿曹植,焦急万分,急忙来见曹丕。

Narrator: Empress Bian, the mother of Cao Pi, receives the distressing news of her youngest son Cao Xiong's tragic suicide. Overwhelmed with grief, she is further alarmed upon discovering that Cao Pi has given orders for the arrest of Cao Zhi, her other son. Consumed by anxiety, Lady Bian rushes to meet her eldest son in an urgent attempt to intervene.

曹丕:(行礼)拜见母后! 请问母后匆匆前来,有什么重要的事情吗?

Cao Pi: (Bowing) Greetings, Mother! What brings you here in such haste? Is there something important?

卞太后:(悲愤)我那两个儿子,一个自杀了,另一个将要被杀,我能不着急吗?

Empress Bian: (Emotionally) Two of my sons, one has taken his own life, and the other's life is in danger. How can I not be worried?

曹丕:(谦恭)我只是派人去询问情况,谁知道四弟竟然就自杀了,我也是心痛不已。

Cao Pi: (Humbly) I only wished to inquire about Cao Xiong's actions. I never intended to harm him. I am also deeply saddened by the circumstances.

卞太后:(哭诉)那么你三弟呢? 他只是有些才气,性格狂放,平时又好饮酒,免不了有些放纵。请你念在一母同胞的情分上,不要把他处死,我以后在九泉之下也就能够瞑目了。

Empress Bian: (Sobbing) And what about your third brother? He has always had that weakness for wine, but we let him go his way out of consideration of his undoubted ability. I hope you will not forget he is your brother and that I bore you both. Spare his life so that I may close my eyes in peace in the nether world.

曹丕:(惭愧)母后误会了。我也爱惜三弟的才气。这次召他前来,只是训诫一下罢了,怎么会杀害他呢? 母后尽管放心,现在请回吧。

Cao Pi: (Ashamed) Mother, you have misunderstood. I also admire his ability, and have no intention of hurting him. But I would reform him. Have no anxiety as to his fate. Please trust me, Mother. Now, please return.

第三幕

Act 3

———

曹植七步成诗逃死劫

Cao Zhi's Miraculous Poem Saves Him from Execution

【人物】 曹丕、曹植、华歆、文臣武将
【Characters】 Cao Pi, Cao Zhi, Hua Xin, Civil and Military Officials
【场景】 王宫内
【Scene】 Inside the Palace
【剧本】
【Script】

旁白:曹丕安抚好卞太后之后,召集大臣们议事。华歆向曹丕献上一计。

Narrator: Cao Pi, after comforting Empress Bian, gathers the ministers for a discussion. Hua Xin proposes a scheme to Cao Pi.

华歆:(小心翼翼)太后是否劝殿下不要诛杀临淄侯?

Hua Xin: (Cautiously) Has Her Majesty advised Your Highness against executing the Lord of Linzi?

曹丕:(失望)是的。

Cao Pi: (Disappointed) Yes.

华歆:(担忧状)临淄侯恃才自傲,如果不除,恐怕会成为以后的祸患。

Hua Xin: (Worried) Lord Linzi is excessively proud and arrogant. If he is spared, he may become a future threat.

曹丕:(面有难色)母命不好违背啊。

Cao Pi: (Reluctant) It's difficult to defy Mother's orders.

华歆:(鬼鬼祟祟)人人都说他才气过人,殿下就考考他的文才。如果他答不上来,就说他诓骗世人,可以把他杀掉;如果他能够对答,就不要杀他,但可进行贬黜。这样谁也没有话说。

Hua Xin: (Slyly) People praise the Lord of Linzi's exceptional talent. Your Highness can test his literary ability. If he fails, accuse him of deceiving others and have him executed. If he succeeds, spare his life but demote him. Thus no one can object.

曹丕:(窃喜)此计甚妙。宣曹植觐见。

Cao Pi: (Secretly pleased) That's a brilliant plan. Summon Cao Zhi.

曹植:(叩首)微臣曹植拜见魏王。

Cao Zhi: (Kowtowing) I, Cao Zhi, humbly greet the King of Wei.

曹丕:你我虽说是兄弟关系,但现在更是君臣的关系,你怎敢蔑视本王?

Cao Pi: Although we are brothers by blood, we now have the king-minister relationship. How dare you disrespect your king?

曹植:微臣不敢。

Cao Zhi: I dare not.

曹丕:先王在世时,你经常夸耀自己文才过人,我对此深表怀疑。现在我就考你一下,命你在七步之内吟诗一首。如果吟得上来,我就饶你一命;如果吟不上来,我要治你死罪,绝不宽恕。

Cao Pi: When our father was alive, you often boasted of your literary talent, which I doubted deeply. Now I will test you. I command you to compose a poem within seven steps. If you succeed, I will spare you your life. If you fail, I will punish you with death, without mercy.

曹植:请魏王出题。

Cao Zhi: Please give me the topic, Your Majesty.

曹丕:我和你是兄弟,就以此为题,但诗中不能出现"兄弟"两字。

Cao Pi: Let's take our brotherhood as the theme, but the word "brother" cannot be mentioned in the poem.

曹植:(略一思索,缓缓地迈出第一步、第二步):煮豆持作羹,漉菽以为汁。(接着迈出第三步……第五步)其在釜下燃,豆在釜中泣。(悲愤地)本是同根生,(第七步)相煎何太急。(曹丕及权臣面面相觑,惊叹不已)。

Cao Zhi: (After a brief thought, he slowly takes the first and second paces): Cooking beans to make a broth, straining the bean juice. (Continuing with the third pace ... the fifth pace) The husk burns beneath the cauldron, Beans weep inside the cauldron. (With sorrow and indignation) Born from the same roots, (the seventh pace) Why rush to scorch each other? (Cao Pi and his ministers exchange astonished glances, amazed by the poem's brilliance)

曹丕:(无奈)既然你能在七步之内作诗,足见有才,我怎么忍心残害手足呢? 死罪可免,但还是要惩戒你不敬之罪,就贬为安乡侯吧。

Cao Pi: (Reluctantly) Since you can compose a poem within seven paces, it proves your talent. How can I bear to harm my own kin? I can spare you your life, but you will be demoted to the Lord of Anxiang.

旁白：由于一直受到曹丕的猜忌和迫害，曹植屡遭贬爵和改换封地，最后忧郁而死，终年四十一岁。

Narrator：Cao Zhi is a victim of Cao Pi's relentless suspicion and persecution. He suffers multiple demotions and frequent transfers to new fiefs. At the age of 41, he succumbs to the weight of his hardships and passes away.

三、故事赏析 Story Analysis

中国古代，由于君王的子嗣众多，经常出现为争王位而兄弟相残的局面，曹丕与曹植也逃不过这个残酷的命运。这反映了封建统治集团内部的残酷斗争。面对曹丕咄咄逼人的杀心和七步吟诗的刁难命题，曹植不愧有着过人的才气，在七步之内吟诗一首，化解了自己的危机，剧中曹丕、曹植、卞太后、华歆等人物的形象和性格特点跃然纸上。

Throughout China's feudal dynasties, the abundance of royal offsprings often led to situations where brothers fought against each other for the throne. This cruel destiny was not exempt from Cao Pi and Cao Zhi, who were both forced to contend with the ruthless struggles within the feudal ruling class. Confronted with Cao Pi's menacing intent to kill and the challenging task of composing a poem in seven paces, Cao Zhi, with his extraordinary talent, proved himself. He skillfully crafted a poem within the given constraints, resolving his own perilous situation. In the play, the characters of Cao Pi, Cao Zhi, Empress Bian, Hua Xin, and others come to life with distinct personalities and traits.

第六节
Section Six

———

乐不思蜀

Indulge in Pleasures and Forget Home

一、故事梗概 Synopsis

魏国邓艾进攻成都，后主刘禅出城投降，蜀汉灭亡。一日，司马昭宴请刘禅，故意安排蜀国的节目，旁边的人都为刘禅亡国感到悲伤，而唯有刘禅却欢乐嬉笑。司马昭问刘禅是否思念蜀地时，刘禅说在这里一样很快乐，自己并不思念蜀地。这就是乐不思蜀的故事。

The Wei general Deng Ai launched an attack on Chengdu, which led to the surrender and downfall of the Shu Han regime. Later, Sima Zhao, a prominent figure in Wei, invited Liu Shan, the last ruler of Shu Han, to a banquet. During the event, performances related to the lost Shu Kingdom were presented, evoking sadness among the attendees except for Liu Shan, who remained joyful and carefree.

When asked if he missed Chengdu, Liu Shan stated that he was content and did not long for his homeland. This story portrays the theme of indulging in pleasures and forgetting one's home.

二、戏剧舞台 Theatre Stages

第一幕

Act 1

————

魏军逼近成都，后主出城受降

The Wei Army Advances Towards Chengdu; The Latter Ruler Surrenders

【人物】 刘禅、谯周、刘谌、众大臣、军士

【Characters】 Liu Shan, Qiao Zhou, Liu Chen, Ministers, Soldiers

【场景】 蜀国宫殿

【Scene】 The Palace of Shu

【剧本】

【Script】

旁白：魏国大将邓艾险出奇兵，暗度阴平，过江油，得绵竹，直奔成都而来。诸葛亮之子诸葛瞻率兵迎敌，战败自杀。成都危急。

Narrator: The Wei army, led by the formidable general Deng Ai, has employed unexpected tactics to cross the Yinping Mountains and capture Jiangyou and Mianzhu. The Wei army swiftly advances towards Chengdu. Zhuge Liang's son, Zhuge Zhan, leads the Shu troops in an attempt to resist but suffers a defeat, and tragically takes his own life. Chengdu is now in imminent danger.

军士：(仓皇急报)邓艾攻取绵竹，诸葛瞻、诸葛亮父子战败殉国了。敌人已到都城。

Soldiers: (Rushing in, panicked) Deng Ai has captured Mianzhu, and Zhuge Zhan and his son Zhuge Shang have been defeated and martyred. The enemy is now at our gates.

刘禅:(惊慌)各位爱卿,谁有退敌良策?

Liu Chan: (Anxious) Dear ministers, does anyone have a strategy to repel the enemy?

众大臣:(议论纷纷)我们现在缺兵少将,难以应敌。如何是好啊?

Ministers: (Discussing) We do not have enough troops to protect the capital. What should we do?

谯周:以臣之见,我们不如投降吧。魏国必定会善待陛下,老百姓也能免受战争之苦。请陛下三思。

Qiao Zhou: In my opinion, it would be better for us to surrender. Surrender to Wei, and Wei people will certainly treat Your Majesty well, and the common people will be spared the hardships of war. I desire Your Majesty to think over this matter.

刘禅:(犹豫)你说的也有几分道理。

Liu Chan: (Hesitant) There is some logic in what you say.

刘谌:(怒骂)苟且偷生之辈,怎配妄议国家大事!

Liu Chen: (Angry outburst) You corrupt pedant, unfit to live among people! How dare you offer such mad advice in a matter concerning the existence of our kingdom?

刘禅:(责备)大臣商议投降,你难道打算让全城百姓惨遭荼毒吗?

Liu Chan: (Reproaching) The ministers have conferred about surrender. Would you like to see the city drenched in blood?

刘谌:(大声)儿臣预计成都还有几万兵马可以抵挡,姜维驻军剑阁,听到消息一定会全力援救。这样内外合力,就可以打退敌兵。陛下怎么能够听从小人之言,轻易丢弃先帝创下的基业呢?

Liu Chen: (Loudly) I believe that we still have numerous legions of soldiers in the city, and Jiang Wei remains undefeated at Saber Pass. He will come to our rescue as soon as he knows our straits. Together we shall surely succeed. Why listen to the words of this snob? Why abandon thus lightly the work of our great forerunner?

刘禅:(呵斥)你还年轻,懂什么。我岂敢逆天而为。

Liu Chan: (Scolding) You are too young to understand it. I would never dare to defy the will of Heaven.

刘谌:(大哭)先帝创立基业不容易,我们怎能轻易丢弃呢?我宁死也不愿受辱。

Liu Chen: (Crying) Is it shameful in one day to throw down all that our ancestors built up with such great labor? I would rather die.

刘禅:(无奈)事已至此,就由谯周起草降书,我们出城投降吧。

Liu Chan: (Helpless) It has come to this point. Qiao Zhou, prepare the formal "Act of Surrender". Let us go out of the city to submit.

第二幕

Act 2

———

刘禅迁居赴洛阳,乐在其中不思归

Liu Shan Relocates to Luoyang; The Lure Makes Him Forget Home

【人物】 司马昭、刘禅、贾充、郤正、军士

【Characters】 Sima Zhao, Liu Shan, Jia Chong, Xi Zheng, Soldiers

【场景】 魏国宫殿

【Scene】 The Palace of Wei

【剧本】

【Script】

旁白：刘禅投降后,司马昭命令他迁到洛阳居住。司马昭对刘禅还是有些放心不下,准备再探探虚实。

Narrator：After Liu Shan surrenders, Sima Zhao orders Liu Shan to relocate to Luoyang. However, Sima Zhao still harbors suspicions towards Liu Shan and plans to further investigate him.

司马昭：刘禅你荒淫无道,近小人,远贤才,治国无能,罪当问斩。

Sima Zhao: Liu Shan, you have indulged in debauchery, favored villains over virtuous men, and governed ineptly. By all rights, your head should be forfeited.

刘禅：(紧张)我,我……

Liu Chan:（Nervously）I, I ...

贾充：蜀国后主虽然不配为一国之君,但是早早就投降,应该赦免他。

Jia Chong: Although the Latter Ruler of Shu is unworthy of being a sovereign, he has surrendered without a struggle, and he now deserves pardon.

司马昭：(点头)有道理。那么便封刘禅为安乐公吧,希望你安安分分做一个降臣。

Sima Zhao:（Nods）That makes sense. Then let Liu Shan be enfeoffed as the Duke of Anle. I hope you will be a loyal vassal and behave yourself.

刘禅：(感激)感谢您的恩赐。

Liu Shan:（Grateful）Thank you for your grace.

司马昭：(高兴)既然如此,今日设宴款待各位大臣,还有蜀国的降臣。

Sima Zhao:（Happily）In that case, today we shall hold a banquet to entertain the ministers and the vassals of Shu.

刘禅：（叩首）臣不胜感激。

Liu Shan:（Kowtowing）I am deeply grateful.

旁白：司马昭命人安排魏国歌舞表演，随同投降的蜀国臣子看到表演后都非常感伤，而刘禅看后却面露喜色；随后又安排蜀国人演奏蜀国的乐曲、跳蜀国舞蹈，蜀臣们不由得想起自己国破家亡，个个泪流满面，而唯独刘禅依旧嬉笑自若。

Narrator： At the banquet, Sima Zhao arranges for Wei's songs and dances to be performed, which saddens the former officials of Shu. However, Liu Shan appears cheerful. Subsequently, Shu's music and dances are performed, and the former Shu officials cannot help but recall their fallen kingdom, and their faces wet with tears. Only Liu Shan remains carefree, laughing as before.

司马昭：你思念蜀地吗？

Sima Zhao: Do you not miss your homeland, Shu?

刘禅：我在这里很快乐，不想念蜀地。

Liu Shan: I felt joyful in this place, and forget about Shu.

郤正：（靠近刘禅，低声地）陛下，您怎么能说不想念蜀地呢？如果等会儿司马昭再问您这个问题，您就哭着回答："先人坟墓，远在蜀地，我没有一天不想念啊！"然后闭上眼睛表达极度的悲痛，司马昭听后一定会允许您回到蜀地。

Xi Zheng:（Approaching Liu Shan, in a low voice）Why did Your Majesty not say you missed Shu? If Sima Zhao asks you again, you can weep and say, "The tombs of my ancestors lie in Shu, and not a day goes by that I don't long for it." Then close your eyes to express deep sorrow. Sima Zhao may allow you to return.

刘禅：（点头）好的，我记住了。

Liu Shan:（Nods）Got it.

司马昭：（再问刘禅）我很高兴你愿意待在洛阳，你真的不思念蜀地吗？

Sima Zhao:（Asking Liu Shan again）I'm glad you are willing to stay in Luoyang. Do you truly not miss Shu?

刘禅：（哭不出来，只好闭目）先人坟墓，远在蜀地，我没有一天不想念啊！

Liu Shan:（Unable to shed tears, just closes his eyes）The tombs of my ancestors lie in Shu, and not a day goes by that I don't long for it.

司马昭：（奇怪）咦？这句话怎么像是郤正说的？

Sima Zhao:（Curiously）Oh? Isn't that what Xi Zheng told you to say?

刘禅：（惊讶地）您怎么知道的？正是郤正教我的。

Liu Shan:（Surprised）How did you know? It is just as you say.

司马昭：（大笑，叹息）想不到刘禅竟糊涂到了这种地步，即使诸葛亮活到现在也不能辅佐他很好地治国理政，更何况是姜维呢。

Sima Zhao:（Laughs and sighs）I never expected Liu Shan to be so clueless. Even if Zhuge Liang were alive today, he wouldn't be able to assist Liu Shan in governing the state properly, let alone Jiang Wei.

贾充：（微笑）他的确糊涂，如果不是这样，殿下您又怎么能吞并蜀国呢？

Jia Chong:（Smiling）He is indeed clueless. If not for that, Your Highness, how could you have conquered Shu?

司马昭：（大笑）哈哈！的确如此，看来我可以放下心了。

Sima Zhao:（Laughs）Haha! Indeed. It seems I can put my mind at ease now.

三、故事赏析 Story Analysis

虽然刘禅已经投降，但司马昭对他仍不放心，决定探一探虚实。酒宴上分别演奏了魏国和蜀国的乐曲，蜀国的降臣都非常伤感，想起国破家亡，个个泪流满面，而唯独刘禅依旧嬉笑自若。在司马昭询问刘禅是否想念蜀地时，刘禅竟然答复在洛阳很快乐，不思念蜀地，逗得众人哈哈大笑，司马昭也就放心任由刘禅去做安乐公了。刘禅投降后的傻态，或许是他身处险境采取的明哲保身的韬晦之计。

Sima Zhao was skeptical of Liu Shan's loyalty after his surrender, and decided to probe his true intentions. During a banquet, the music of Wei and Shu was performed, which evoked deep sadness among the former officials of Shu as they reminisced about their fallen kingdom. However, Liu Shan remained lighthearted and continued to laugh. When Sima Zhao questioned Liu Shan about his feelings for Shu, Liu Shan surprisingly expressed contentment in his feelings situation and claimed not to miss his homeland. This response elicited laughter from the crowd, and Sima Zhao felt more assured, allowing Liu Shan to assume the title of the Duke of Anle. One possible explanation for Liu Shan's behavior is that he was deliberately feigning foolishness in order to conceal his true intentions in the face of adversity.

汉中成语典故戏剧悦读

Theatrical Delights: Idioms from Hanzhong

一笑千金

The Beacon Fires that Laughter Lit

一、故事梗概 Synopsis

西周末期,周幽王为博褒姒一笑,下令点燃了烽火台,号令诸侯带兵勤王。褒姒见此情景后竟然笑了,周幽王为此很高兴。为博褒姒欢心,周幽王故技重施,多次下令点燃烽火。诸侯带兵勤王,发现没有敌情,竟然是周幽王在作乐,他们被戏弄了,多次后也就不相信了。后来,当犬戎进攻镐京时,诸侯看到烽火后以为仍是周幽王在胡闹,就不再带兵勤王。结果,犬戎攻破镐京,杀死了周幽王,西周灭亡。

During the late Western Zhou Dynasty, Emperor Zhou You, in his quest to elicit a smile from his beloved Bao Si, ordered to ignite the beacon fires atop the watchtowers. This action signaled the feudal vassals to gather their troops and defend the kingdom. Surprisingly,

Bao Si found the scene amusing, which brought great joy to Emperor Zhou You. In an attempt to win Bao Si's favor, the emperor repeated this act multiple times, even though it was not necessary. The feudal vassals eventually realized that Emperor Zhou You was only using the beacon fires to entertain Bao Si, and they stopped believing in the alarms. Later, when the Quanrong attacked Haojing, the vassals saw the beacon fires but assumed it was another jest, and they did not rally their troops to defend the emperor. As a result, the Quanrong successfully invaded Haojing, killing Emperor Zhou You and leading to the downfall of the Western Zhou Dynasty.

二、戏剧舞台 Theatre Stages

第一幕

Act 1

——

褒姒郁郁寡欢，幽王百思难解

Emperor Zhou You's Confusion About Bao Si's Melancholy

【人物】 周幽王、褒姒

【Characters】 Emperor Zhou You, Bao Si

【场景】 王宫

【Scene】 Inside the Palace

【剧本】

【Script】

旁白：褒姒进宫后，一直没笑过。这让非常宠爱她的周幽王非常苦恼。

Narrator: Bao Si never smiles in the palace, which deeply troubles Emperor Zhou You who favors her greatly.

周幽王：爱妃,你怎么了?

Emperor Zhou You: My darling, what's troubling you?

褒姒：臣妾没事,大王。

Bao Si: It's nothing, Your Majesty.

周幽王：爱妃,到底何事让你如此不开心呢?

Emperor Zhou You: My dear, what on earth is causing you such sadness?

褒姒：你不会明白的。

Bao Si: You wouldn't understand.

周幽王：(自言自语)唉,如何才能让寡人的爱妃高兴起来呢?

Emperor Zhou You: (Speaking to himself) Ah, how can I bring happiness back to my beloved?

第二幕

Act 2

——

幽王千金求妃笑,虢石父献计戏诸侯

Emperor Zhou You Rewards a Thousand Pieces of Gold to Quest for Bao Si's Smile; Guo Shifu Suggests to Tease the Vassals

【人物】 周幽王、虢石父

【Characters】 Emperor Zhou You, Guo Shifu

【场景】 宫殿内

【Scene】 Inside the Palace

【剧本】

【Script】

旁白：周幽王一定要让褒姒笑一笑,决定通过悬赏征求办法。

Narrator: Determined to make Bao Si smile, Emperor Zhou You decides to offer a reward to solicit ideas.

周幽王:不管是什么人,凡是能让褒后一笑者,赏赐千金。

Emperor Zhou You: Whoever can make the Queen smile will be rewarded with one thousand pieces of gold.

虢石父:陛下与王后同游骊山,放起狼烟,附近诸侯必定会带领援兵赶来,随后发现没有敌兵,王后见此情景必笑无疑矣。

Guo Shifu: Your Majesty, if you and the Queen visit Mount Li together and light the beacon fires, the nearby vassals will undoubtedly bring their troops to your aid. When they arrive and find no enemy forces, the Queen will certainly laugh at the scene.

周幽王:此计甚好!

Emperor Zhou You: That is an excellent plan!

第三幕

Act 3

———

第一次戏诸侯,幽王博得妃子笑

Emperor Zhou You's First Jest to Tease His Vassals and Win His Beloved's Smile

【人物】 周幽王、褒姒、诸侯甲、诸侯乙

【Characters】 Emperor Zhou You, Bao Si, Vassal A, Vassal B

【场景】 骊山烽火台

【Scene】 Beacon tower on Mount Li

【剧本】

【Script】

旁白:周幽王认为虢石父的办法很好,就带着褒姒去骊山游玩。

Narrator: Emperor Zhou You thinks Guo Shifu's idea is excellent, so he takes Bao Si to Mount Li for a visit.

周幽王：爱妃，今天寡人一定要让你高兴起来。

Emperor Zhou You: My darling, today I will surely bring a smile to your face.

褒姒：能有什么高兴的事呢？

Bao Si: What could possibly make me happy?

周幽王：你看，这是寡人给你打下的江山。

Emperor Zhou You: Look, this is the realm I have conquered for you.

褒姒：大王，我不喜欢这些。

Bao Si: Your Majesty, I do not find joy in these things.

周幽王：爱妃，你看！

Emperor Zhou You: Darling, just look!

旁白：周幽王下令点燃烽火。狼烟四起，诸侯看到后带领兵马匆匆赶来。

Narrator: Emperor Zhou You orders the beacon fires to be lit. Upon seeing them, the vassals swiftly lead their troops to rush over.

诸侯甲、诸侯乙：（弯腰行礼）大王，您的将士将为您而战，但怎么没发现敌情呢？

Vassal A, Vassal B: (Bowing) Your Majesty, we are ready to fight for you, but we haven't encountered any signs of the enemy.

周幽王：无事，一切平安，你们一路辛苦了，回去吧。

Emperor Zhou You: There is no need to worry. Everything is peaceful. You have all traveled a long way, so you may return now.

褒姒：（笑）大王，他们真好笑，我喜欢。

Bao Si: (Laughing) Your Majesty, they are quite amusing. I enjoy it.

周幽王：爱妃喜欢就好，以后经常给你看！

Emperor Zhou You: As long as you like, I will continue to entertain you like this in the future.

褒姒:谢大王,那再好不过了。

Bao Si: Thank you, Your Majesty. It couldn't be better.

第四幕
Act 4

———

第二次戏诸侯,幽王再博妃子笑

Emperor Zhou You's Second Jest to Amuse His Vassals and Once Again Win His Beloved's Smile

【人物】 周幽王、褒姒、诸侯甲、诸侯乙

【**Characters**】 Emperor Zhou You, Bao Si, Vassal A, Vassal B

【场景】 骊山烽火台

【**Scene**】 Beacon tower on Mount Li

【剧本】

【**Script**】

旁白:周幽王见褒姒又不高兴,就决定故技重演。

Narrator: Upon seeing that Bao Si is unhappy again, Emperor Zhou You decides to repeat the old trick.

周幽王:爱妃,今天心情怎么样呢?

Emperor Zhou You: Darling, how are you feeling today?

褒姒:陛下,若是再能目睹那烽火燃起及诸侯狼狈之状,我就很开心了。

Bao Si: Your Majesty, if I could witness the beacon fires again and see the lords in a state of chaos, I would be very happy.

周幽王:哈哈哈,我深知你心,爱妃稍等。

Emperor Zhou You: Hahaha! I know your heart well, my dear. Please wait a moment.

诸侯甲、诸侯乙：大王，请问这次是何方有战事？

Vassal A , Vassal B: Your Majesty, may we ask where the battle is this time?

周幽王：无事，尔等退下吧。

Emperor Zhou You: There is no battle. You may all withdraw.

褒姒：哇，果然能再次看到这么有趣的事。

Bao Si: Wow! Once again, I get to witness such an amusing spectacle.

周幽王：爱妃可喜欢？

Emperor Zhou You: My dear, do you find it pleasing?

褒姒：臣妾很喜欢，谢谢大王。

Bao Si: I really enjoyed it. Thank you, Your Majesty.

周幽王：喜欢就好。

Emperor Zhou You: I am glad you liked it.

诸侯甲：（退下后，自言自语）我从未见过这样的王！

Vassal A: (Withdrawing and muttering to himself) I have never seen a king like him!

诸侯乙：（摇头自语）亡国不可避免啊！

Vassal B: (Shaking his head and muttering) The downfall of our kingdom is unavoidable!

第五幕

Act 5

———

多次戏弄酿苦果，最终国破又家亡

Repeated Teasing Brings Bitter Consequences, Leading to the Empire's Collapse

【人物】 周幽王、褒姒、虢石父、诸侯甲、诸侯乙、犬戎

【Characters】 Emperor Zhou You, Bao Si, Guo Shifu, Vassal A,

Vassal B, Quanrong

【场景】 骊山烽火台

【Scene】 Beacon tower on Mount Li

【剧本】

【Script】

旁白：犬戎领兵攻到骊山脚下。

Narrator：Quanrong's troops advance to the foot of Mount Li.

犬戎：幽王无道，我们要取而代之，今天讨伐之。

Quan Rong: Emperor Zhou You is tyrannical. We must replace

him. Today, we shall launch an attack.

虢石父：(声色慌张)大事不好，犬戎带兵打过来了。

Guo Shifu: (Anxiously) This is bad! Quanrong is approaching

with their troops.

周幽王：(大惊失色)快，快，快放狼烟，召集各路诸侯带兵救

寡人。

Emperor Zhou You: (Freaked) Quick, quickly, light the beacon

fires! Summon the vassals to gather their troops and rescue me.

褒姒：(急切地)大王，诸侯怎么还没来呢？

Bao Si: (Urgently) Your Majesty, why haven't they arrived yet?

周幽王：(故作镇定)稍等稍等，诸侯马上就来。

Emperor Zhou You: (Feigning calm) Just wait a little longer. The

vassals will come soon.

诸侯甲：狼烟又起来了，去不去呢？

Vassal A: The beacon fires have been lit again. Should we go

or not?

诸侯乙：一定又是周幽王在戏弄我们，不用管。

Vassal B: It's probably another prank by our king. Just ignore it.

诸侯甲：你说得对，不用管。

Vassal A: You are right. Let it be.

犬戎：诸侯不会再来了，投降吧。

Quan Rong: Your vassals won't come anymore. Just surrender.

周幽王：（垂头丧气）唉！我们要亡了。

Emperor Zhou You:（Dejected）Alas! We are doomed.

三、故事赏析 Story Analysis

作为国家的统治者，要推行仁政，守信，不要愚弄人民，否则便会引起民愤，给国家带来灭顶之灾。对于我们个人而言，如果在平时失信于人，当危难发生的时候，就得不到别人的帮助。诚信是一种珍贵的品质，"人无信不立"，一个没有诚信的人可能会身败名裂。

As leaders of a nation, it is essential to implement the policy of benevolence and maintain trustworthiness. This means avoiding any deception towards the people, as it can ignite public resentment and lead to the downfall of the country. On a personal level, if we are not trustworthy, we will eventually find ourselves without the support of others when we face hardships. Integrity is a kind of precious quality. A person without trustworthiness cannot succeed. Those who compromise their integrity will ultimately suffer the ruin of their reputation.

第二节
Section Two

———

廉泉让水

Lianquan River and Rang River

一、故事梗概 Synopsis

南北朝时，梁州的范柏年到京城拜见皇帝，宋明帝与他闲谈时，问他当地有没有像广州的贪泉一样的泉水。面对一语双关的问询，范柏年思考后答复说当地没有贪泉，恰恰相反，当地有廉泉，也有让水，而自己就居住在廉泉和让水之间，暗示自己为政清廉，受到了皇帝的赞赏。

During the period of the Northern and Southern Dynasties, Fan Bainian, an official from Liangzhou, visited the capital city to meet Emperor Ming of Song. The emperor engaged in a casual conversation with Fan and asked if there was a spring in Liangzhou similar to the Tan Spring in Guangzhou. (The "Tan" refers to both the name of the spring and corrupt officials.) Faced with this cleverly worded question,

218

Fan Bainian pondered and replied that there was no Tan Spring in Liangzhou. In fact, quite the opposite, there was a Lianquan River and the Rang River. (The "Lian" represented incorruptibility, and the "Rang" represented courtliness.) Fan implied that he lived between the Lianquan River and the Rang River, suggesting his own integrity and honesty as an official. This response earned him praise from the emperor.

二、戏剧舞台 Theatre Stages

独幕戏
One-Act Play

【人物】 宋明帝、范柏年、近侍

【Characters】 Emperor Ming of Song, Fan Bainian, Bodyguards

【场景】 皇宫

【Scene】 Inside the Palace

【剧本】

【Script】

旁白:南北朝时期,梁州太守派遣范柏年到京城觐见皇上,宋明帝在听完汇报后与他进行交谈。

Narrator: Fan Bainian, an official of Liangzhou, is sent to the capital to meet Emperor Ming of Song. After hearing his report, the emperor engages in a conversation with him.

宋明帝:(淡淡地)一方水土养一方人,各个地方有不同的风土人情。爱卿,你以为如何?

Emperor Ming of Song: (Casually) Each region has its own unique characteristics shaped by its land and people. Bainian, what are your thoughts on this matter?

范柏年：(附和)皇上所言极是。

Fan Bainian: (Agreeing) Your Majesty, your words are absolutely true.

宋明帝：(突然)广州有个贪泉,你知道否?

Emperor Ming of Song: (Suddenly) Is there a Tan Spring in Guangzhou?

范柏年：(谨慎)微臣略有耳闻。

Fan Bainian: (Cautiously) I have heard a little about it, Your Majesty.

宋明帝：(颇有兴趣)愿闻其详。

Emperor Ming of Song: (Quite interested) Please tell me more.

范柏年：(平静)在广州石门这个地方,有一眼泉水,如果谁饮了泉中之水,就会变得爱钱如命,贪得无厌,因此当地老百姓就给它取名"贪泉"。前朝广州的官员大多贪污腐化,可能与此有关。

Fan Bainian:(Calmly) In Stone Gate, Guangzhou, there is a spring. Those who drink its water become obsessed with money and insatiable greed. Therefore, the locals named it "Tan Spring". This might be related to the rampant corruption among former officials in Guangzhou.

宋明帝：(严肃状)梁州是否有这样的泉水?

Emperor Ming of Song: (Seriously) Does Liangzhou have such a spring?

范柏年：(认真地)据微臣所知,梁州没有叫贪泉的泉水。

Fan Bainian: (Seriously) To the best of my knowledge, Liangzhou does not have a spring like Tan Spring.

宋明帝：(追问)那梁州有什么著名的泉水吗?

Emperor Ming of Song:(Questioning further) Are there any famous springs in Liangzhou?

范柏年:(思索片刻)梁州城外有两条河,地处一南一北,老百姓把南边的叫作廉泉,把北边的叫作让水。

Fan Bainian: (Pondering for a moment) Outside the city of Liangzhou, there are two rivers. One is in the south, known as Lianquan River, and the other is in the north, known as Rang River, according to the locals.

宋明帝:(看似关心)那爱卿家居何地?

Emperor Ming of Song: (Appearing concerned) Where is your residence?

范柏年:(谦逊)微臣之家地处廉泉与让水之间,在此地居住已有三代了。

Fan Bainian: (Humbly) I reside between the Lianquan River and the Rang River. My family has been living there for three generations.

宋明帝:(质疑)此话当真?

Emperor Ming of Song: (Doubtful) Is that so?

范柏年:(紧张)不敢有半分虚假。

Fan Bainian: (Nervously) I would never dare to utter a falsehood.

宋明帝:(高兴)甚好。(试探)爱卿来京一趟不易,多住几日游玩之后再回去吧。

Emperor Ming of Song: (Delighted) Excellent. (Testing) Since it is not easy for you to come to the capital, why don't you stay a little longer and go sightseeing before returning?

范柏年:(叩首)谢皇上,微臣还有公务在身,今天就准备动身回去了。微臣告退。

Fan Bainian: (Kowtowing) Thank you, Your Majesty. I have official duties to attend to, so I must depart today. I shall take my leave.

三、故事赏析 Story Analysis

在这场独幕戏中，宋明帝对范柏年的问话，既有一语双关的深意，又有步步紧追的严厉；范柏年的回答既说明他任职之地民风淳朴，又暗示自己为政清廉，巧妙机智，无懈可击。两人的谈话虽然波澜不惊，却也是暗藏风险，同时也充分表现了汉语的博大精深和绝妙精彩。

In this one-act play, Emperor Ming of Song's questioning of Fan Bainian serves as a test of Fan's integrity and wit. The emperor's carefully crafted questions contain hidden meanings. Fan's responses not only demonstrate the simplicity of the local customs in his region but also imply his own integrity and cleverness, showcasing his impeccable wit. The conversation between the emperor and Fan is calm on the surface, but it is imbued with hidden risks. Furthermore, the story exemplifies the beauty of the Chinese language, revealing its immense depth and richness.

参考文献

References

[1] 陈岩,王秀娟. 走进中国文化:英文版[M]. 天津:南开大学出版
    社,2011.

[2]《二十四史》编委会. 二十四史:文白对照精华版[M]. 北京:线
    装书局,2014.

[3] 罗贯中. 三国演义[M]. 北京:人民文学出版社,2018.

[4] 许渊冲. 唐诗:上:汉英对照[M]. 北京:海豚出版社,2015.

[5] 许渊冲. 唐诗:下:汉英对照[M]. 北京:海豚出版社,2015.

[6] 许渊冲. 许渊冲译汉魏六朝诗:汉英对照[M]. 北京:中译出版
    社,2009.

[7] 叶郎,朱良志. 中国文化读本[M]. 北京:外语教学与研究出版
    社,2008.

[8] 叶郎,朱良志. 中国文化读本:英文版[M]. 北京:外语教学与研
    究出版社,2008.

[9] 曾小珊. 魅力汉中[M]. 成都:西南交通大学出版社,2019.

后记
Postscript

本书由陕西省社会科学界联合会立项并资助（项目编号：2021SKZZ024），同时也是2018年陕西省社会科学基金项目（项目编号：2018M16）的后续研究成果。

This book was approved and funded by the Shaanxi Federation of Social Sciences (Project No. 2021SKZZ024), and it is also the follow-up research result of the Shaanxi Social Science Fund Project in 2018 (Project No. 2018M16).

本书立足于陕西省汉中市，对两汉三国等时期与汉中有关的历史故事、成语典故进行诠释和戏剧改编。这既是对地方历史文化的宣传和推广，更是对中华优秀传统文化的弘扬。

The book interprets and dramatizes local historical stories, especially idioms and allusions of the Han and Three Kingdoms, which are related to Hanzhong City, Shaanxi Province. It is a valuable resource for promoting local history and culture, as well as fostering a deeper understanding of Chinese outstanding traditional culture.

本书可以作为宣传地方文化和传统文化的普及读物，也可以作为学校开展第二课堂实践教学的重要资料,同时也可以作为初中及高中学生英语课外阅读的拓展教材,以及大学英语通识课教学和阅读的材料。本书也可以作为中国文化宣传材料,便于对中国文化感兴趣的读者阅读。

The book not only serves as a popular reading material to promote local culture and traditional Chinese culture, but also holds significant value as a resource for schools to conduct second classroom practice teaching. Moreover, it can be used as an expanded textbook for junior and senior high school students' English reading, as well as a teaching and reading material for college English general education courses. As a kind of Chinese culture publicity material, the book is also well-suited for readers interested in exploring Chinese culture.

本书的写作和出版得到了陕西理工大学的大力支持和资助,在此表示感谢。同时,感谢我校文学院 2018 级、2019 级研究生,外国语学院 2018 级研究生和马克思主义学院 2019 级研究生对部分资料的搜集和整理。

I extend my heartfelt gratitude to Shaanxi University of Technology for its unwavering support and generous funding towards the writing and publication of this book. I would also like to express my appreciation to the graduate students from the classes of 2018 and 2019 of the School of Arts, the class of 2018 from the School of Foreign Languages, and the class of 2019 from the School of Marxism in our university. Their dedicated efforts in collecting and organizing materials have been instrumental in bringing this project to fruition.

由于笔者水平有限,书中难免有不足之处,敬请读者批评指正。

I am aware that the book may have some flaws due to my limited level. I would welcome any constructive criticism and corrections from readers, which will undoubtedly contribute to further improving the quality of this work.